# Getting Acquainted

César Grinstein

Translation, correction and new ideas
Alan Grintsein

## Extensive dedications, small talent

"In every achievement that you have obtained, you will always have counted on the help of someone"
*Althea Gibson - First black tennis player to win Wimbledon*

To begin, I need to make a confession: Writing requires a talent and tenacity that exceed me. I learned that when writing this book. It was more than two years of thinking, almost every night before I went to sleep, what would be the phrases that would allow me to express my ideas more fully. Needless to say, these reflections brought me closer to insomnia than to expository clarity.

That is why from now on, surely, all my activity as a writer will be reduced to a few e-mails and a few end of the year greetings. But never again a book.

I will not have, then, new opportunities to thank in writing or to consecrate my efforts. I better be careful, have a good memory and a better heart. The less talent, the more extensive the dedications have to be. If I thought that this book of mine is just the first in a long list, I would be encouraged to be lighter in thanking and more greedy in dedicating. But, I repeat, it will be the only one. More by disability than by desire.

So I start the path of exordiums and recognitions, with the fear of completing only half. Maybe with time, if I reread what is written, I will find it unfair or, at least, forgetful. Many times remembering is more unjust than forgetting. I already apologize for such inequities.

I started the Spanish version of this book at the end of the year 2000. My father was alive and was one of the first to know about my literary plans. I know he was proud of my effort. His life suddenly ended, his departure took us by surprise. He could not read my finished book. It's my old man, then, the first on the list of acknowledgments and dedications. I thank him for being my first teacher, my first master. A very important part of what I teach in my courses, I learned from him. It is to you dad that I dedicate this book in the first place. I love you.

My grandmother Lola was one of the people I most loved in my life. His portentous kindness, his affectionate voice and his cheerful laugh constantly inhabit my soul. His presence was the best gift. I always knew that if I wrote a book, I would dedicate it to her.

My mom left us recently, just the day Alan, my son and his youngest grandson, graduated from Washington & Lee University. Life gives us and takes us away. Until the last moment of his life, my mother dedicated herself to take care of her children. My sister and I were the reason for her life. Mom, I know you deserved a better book, but I dedicate this one to you with all my love.

I was born on Mother's Day in 1959. I grew up in Argentina. I knew the delights and the horrors of that circumstance. I had a very happy childhood, merit that my parents share with my grandmothers Lola and Rosa and with my great aunt María. I was a happy teenager and I declare myself happy in my adult life. I love soccer and I have had the privilege of watching Rojitas, Maradona and Riquelme play for Boca Junios, my favorite team. I am happy to count friends for hundreds. All of them, without exception, are in this book. Remembering them is a way to tell who I am and to thank them for helping me to forge my character and my identity. It also constitutes a strict act of justice, since they are the involuntary collaborators of this book.

As a student of the Bachelor of Economics, I had great teachers. I highlight Luisa Montuschi, Ana Martirena, Juan Carlos De Pablo and Juan Carlos Cresto. And to the dear professor Teresa Casparri de Rodríguez, from whom I had already learned Statistics during high school and I found it again, for my luck and benefit, in Mathematics for Economists. Thanks to them for their wisdom.

I received an economist's degree in July 1984. Soon after, the beloved professor Guido Di Tella, a person of enormous generosity and intelligence, offered me to be his deputy in the Chair of Theory of Economic Growth, of which I had been student little time before. Suddenly I was, at the age of 25 years at the head of a course at the Faculty of Economic Sciences at the University of Buenos Aires. Few challenges would be bigger for me.

Then I started a teaching career that lasted for about ten years. I was fortunate to win a position as Professor of Microeconomics and then of Macroeconomics at the University of Buenos Aires.

Thanks to the help of Professor Di Tella, I was able to get the MIT to accept me as Visiting Scholar. Professor Alan White sent me an invitation and I went to Cambridge - MA. Between 1993 and 1995 I had the opportunity to meet great professors, among whom I highlight Peter Senge, John Van Maanen, Arnoldo Hax, Daniel Schön and Edgar Schein.
Trying to understand more about the companies and business organizations, I studied Ontology of Language. In the hands of Rafael Echeverría I became a Professional Coach. Rafael was the first to show me the importance of language in the lives of human beings. Rafael, I thank you for having existed in my life.

Working in business organizations I have learned a lot more than what I have taught. My experiences leading educational programs, courses and seminars in several countries and for a large number of companies, constitute a learning that I value as the greatest of treasures. My infinite gratitude to all those whom I call affectionately, my students. They are a constant source of challenge and inspiration. Many of the questions that my dear students have asked me have been the beginning of endless explorations. Walking the roads that they illuminate me, I learn at every moment.

Already in the end of these acknowledgements, I have the most important: Says my friend Alejandro Dolina, a very famous argentine writer, that everything men do has the sole purpose of getting the love of the beloved woman. I first saw Alejandra one September afternoon in 1984 and since then my heart belongs to her. Ale is a light of beauty, sweetness, love, affection, kindness, understanding and companionship that descended upon me. I try every day to deserve her love. She is one of the reasons of my life. Many times she accompanied me, in silence, while I struggled with my inexperience to finish a sentence. Other times, a word from her was what kept me going. Finally we did it, "Amore". Thank you.

As if all her love was not enough, Alejandra gave me Kevin and Alan. My children are the other great reason of my life and the most extraordinary blessing I have ever had. For them I live and I am happy. They make every moment a celebration. Kevin and Alan, all the words of the Universe are not enough to say thank you for the love you give me. Being his dad has justified my existence.

Well, that's it. I will never write a book again. Maybe it was not enough, but my heart is in each line. I hope you know how to excuse so many dedications. More for incompetence than for decision, here ends my career as a writer. I confess that I enjoyed the effort.

And already in the last step, at the moment of finishing the last sentence, an idea assails me that is at the same time consolation: if the task is accomplished, maybe now I will not suffer from insomnia again.

César Grinstein
Mar del Plata - Argentina.
January 1, 2019

# Preface

## Words' Power

It was 1987 and I was in New York City. I had just come back to the hotel. I cannot quite remember where from, nor could I confirm the plans I had for the evening. Most likely, my wife, Alejandra, and I were just going to enjoy a simple dinner at the hotel we were staying in. We were young, just married, inexperienced and, back then, Manhattan was not such a safe place to wonder around during the night.

I should confess, when I am traveling, I usually turn the TV on as soon as I walk into the hotel room. I do so urged by my desire of feeling included in the events of the city I am visiting. Generally, a tourist lives somewhat secluded from the daily life happenings and, except during considerable catastrophes, ends up ignoring a good portion of what is going on.
Then, I use the TV as a way of getting informed. Normally, I put on some news channel, and then leave it on while I take care of other trivial issues.
But, that night, while I was swapping looking for ABC, something stopped me for a moment. CBS was airing an episode of a show I had never seen before. Its music and picture caught my attention immediately. It showed the City covered in fog, under pastel colors, with a strange beauty. A young woman, Linda Hamilton, as I ended up finding out, was covered by the arms of a large man with long hair. We could only see the man's back, and he was wearing a cape.

The scene was quite strange; there was something off with the man. He looked like a medieval Prince in the middle of a modern metropolis. However, the most surprising component was yet to be revealed. As the camera moved around the couple, the man's front side became visible. This man had a lion's face.

The Beauty and the Beast. The everlasting love legend between a beautiful woman and a beast, told in a modern, urban version. It was the love story between Catherine, an attractive, risky New York prosecutor, and Vincent, a lion-man with great strength, fine manners and a wide culture. I could not look away from the TV for the next hour. Not just that; I became a fan of the show. Back in Buenos Aires, I happily discovered there was a channel promising to show its pilot in the very next days.

It is not my intention to present an essay on my TV tastes. However, I want to bring focus to the story this show told. The legend of the Beauty and the Beast, besides the fantasy and adventure in it, encloses a mysterious and hopeful message. It shows us love's transformative power.

Almost every culture has a similar tale. Stories making us see love pays off, and comprehension, tenderness, being considerate with others, along with a total respect for own values, provoke unimaginable transformations. Catherine's love calmed Vincent's beastly spirit. Vincent's love made Catherine more courageous. As I watched the show, I could not stop thinking we all are one or the other at many points throughout our lives.

Many years have gone by since that night in New York, many flowers have flourished during different springs, and many lessons have I learnt since then. But, the caption rounding up each episode is still branded in my mind. Ron Perlman, aka Vincent, used to say in a tender, yet aphonic voice: "And, though we cannot be together, we will never be apart."

This book attempts to pick up much from this legend. There are two matters I regard as significant in the story. They both inspire every chapter that follows. First, the unbreakable trust in believing to find a way for overcoming the challenges set ahead, no matter what. Vincent faces his destiny with a conviction and values worthy of a hero. Responding with actions to the challenge before him. Without giving up his supreme values.

My dear friend, Alejandro Dolina, says a hero's job is not to dodge his, mostly, tragic destiny, but to fulfill it. His values allow him to turn his problems into challenges.

Second, I like to think human relationships are mutually transformative. The power of the human word, the power of conversations, is always present and has a leading role in people relationships. And, amongst every human relation, there is no doubt love is the mutually transformative relation par excellence. Capable of turning a lion-man, a beast, into a beautiful, sweet and adorable being, who accomplishes to tame the animal inside him. Capable of turning a woman overwhelmed by her fears into a fearless amazon that does not think twice before facing the dangers before her.

Throughout my career as a consultant, I have come to understand human relations are built with words. Expressing it might result obvious, but I can attest we often forget about it in practice.
Then, the following question rises: What makes a human relationship successful? Is it about saying nice phrases, or being kind, or perhaps saying, "I love you" through and through? I believe it is rather not likely to be this way. I have no doubts a specific word said in a particular moment can determine the destiny of a relationship. An insult, or an honest love declaration may set the way two people ought to get along forever. But, it is not in words themselves, without a context or meaning, where the transformative force lies. The true transformative power lies within conversations. And conversations are not mere collections of random sounds said out loud. Conversations are the articulation of a combination of words, said with a purpose and meaning, serving a goal and leading to action.

The human word only exists in the context of a conversation. The sound is not a word if not attached with an intention. The human word has an intention, works for an interest, answers to values, aims to objectives, and leads to actions.
Then, and only then, within the context of human conversations, the WORD acquires a great transformative power. Human beings have within the word, the most powerful tool we can ever imagine. All human experience, history as a whole, is the result of the transformative power of words.

Wizards are well aware of such power. Surely, more than once we have heard some of them claim "Abracadabra!" when trying their tricks on some stage. The expression is the prelude, or better yet the order, for magic to happen, for a handkerchief to turn into a rose.
Interestingly, the word chosen to invoke the transformation is not a random sound. Abracadabra has its history. One worth telling.

Many centuries ago, the Aramaic used to discuss their issues in meetings that gathered the members of their community. They would talk about different courses of action, and decisions were made. When the meetings were over, the main speaker would always finish with the same phrase: "Avrah kha dabhrah".
The phrase translates into something close to "I believe in what I say" or "May it happen" (taking into account the difference between modern English and old Aramaic). With this, they sought to highlight words are meant to lead to actions, that whatever they arranged at the meetings should happen. It was a sort of meeting closure useful as a reminder, to "make it happen".
During the Aramaean captivity in Persia, the magicians of the court took the phrase and turned it into "Abracadabra". And they started using it to "make it happen", to turn the handkerchief into a rose. There still are many magicians nowadays claiming "Abracadabra!" when performing their tricks, some of them probably not knowing why they say it.

The story of the word "Abracadabra" reminds us and makes us aware of the great transformative power of the human word. Each of us has the possibility to try shape the world in a way that satisfies us, makes us comfortable, makes us happy.
Much closer in time, during the first half of the XIX Century, Walt Whitman, the father of North American literature, claimed in "Leaves of Grass" that words and ideas can change the world indeed.

Well then, here we are. You and I. Making this effort of learning the transformative power of the word to try change the world. Acknowledging human beings depend on words to establish relationships. Understanding those relationships originate in an exchange of words, leading to the coordination of our actions.

The following chapters mean to explore the power of the word, the power of conversations. Essentially, the great power of Human Relationships. Like every kind of power, it comes from the capacity to generate actions. Otherwise, what is power if not the capacity to generate effective actions in a certain domain of action? But, like every capacity to generate actions, aka ability, it has to be learnt. It is not just given to us. We have to acquire it through reflection and practice.

There is much to learn. Relating with other human beings is an art that poses difficult challenges. It is composed by concepts easy to learn, by extremely hard to use. It requires hard work. But, there is a substantial reward: acquiring the skill to manage the transformative power of the word and human relationships.

So there we go. With the hero's spirit, which is also the apprentice's. Then, the beginning will be embarking on the apprentice's path. There are fewer ways more promising to achieve an effective conversation, than tackling it as an apprentice, as someone willing to discover the unknown.

If we accomplish it, we would have given the first step. We will have opened the door to a world with almost infinite possibilities. Given that when we participate in a conversation with the humbleness and curiosity of that who wishes to learn, we will be much closer to achieving effective relationships with others. The transformative power of the word will help us to reach it.

And, if we do not accomplish it, if we do not reach a total agreement, even in failure we will be much more prepared to understand that, as humans, "though we cannot be together, we will never be apart."

# Introduction

I still neatly remember the day my mother gave me that present. It was a sheet with a blue background and white stripes that gave shape to an arc. This pattern was used to highlight a title, "Desiderata". I was ten years old and I was playing by myself in my room, like I usually did. Mom started reading to me the text with the enthusiasm of a reader that hopes to generate a meaningful impact on the listener. Let me say she achieved her goal.

"Placidly walk in between noise and hurry, and remember the peace that can be found in silence. As long as it is possible, and without giving up, try to get along with everyone. Speak your truth in a quiet and clear way. And listen to everyone else, even the clumsy and ignorant ones, because they too have a story to tell. Avoid aggressive and noisy people, as they annoy our spirits. If you compare yourself to other people, you will become vain and embittered, because there will always be bigger and smaller people than yourself. Enjoy your successes as much as your plans. Stay interested in your own path, as humble it might be; it is a blissful treasure on the fortuitous change of times. Be ware when making business, because the world is full of deceit. But do not let that blind you to its virtue, which does exist. In many places, there are many people that make an effort to reach noble ideals. Life is filled with heroism. Be true to yourself. Specially, do not pretend to have affection, and do not be cynical in love. Amidst aridness and disappointments, love is perennial like weeds. Meekly take experience's advice, letting go off youth's grace. Cultivate your spirit's strength so it may protect you from sudden adversities. Many fears rise from fatigue and loneliness. With sane discipline, be benign with yourself. You are a creature of the Universe, not any less than trees and stars. You have a right to be here. And it might or might not be clear to you, but the Universe keeps moving as it should. Therefore, try to be in peace with God, in whatever form you may conceive him. And whichever your jobs and aspirations might be, keep peace with your soul in life's boisterous confusion.

Even with all your faults, farces and failures, the world still is beautiful. Be cautious. Make an effort to be happy."

It was not only the beauty and wisdom I found in those words what made such an impact on me. There was something else: a small print stating "found in the Church of Saint Paul of Baltimore, in 1693."

"Almost three hundred years!" – I told myself- understanding, despite my young age, how current those claims and advises were.

Today, I am fifty eight years old. On one of the walls in my office, with that blue somewhat fainted, but undaunted present, the "Desiderata" phrases are like a lighthouse I use to orient myself. When I started writing this book, I proposed to honor the philosophy around them. I believe we live in times that need those reflections. I suspect they are tremendously current still.

Juan Manuel Serrat, a famous Spanish composer, sings "there is no other time than the one we live in." I rejoice in thinking he is right. I believe the ability of accepting the world's temporality and facticity shows a sign of wisdom.

Nonetheless, this should not be seen as an invitation to renounce to the search of new realities. Along with the world that surrounds us, and that in many occasions we cannot change, we can always find room for possibilities. Such room is composed by everything that has not happened yet, what we can change and even for what we still need to create.

It is this room for possibilities what gives birth to the thoughts expressed in this book. It is my definite conviction that humans are not fatal but contingent what takes me to overcome my clumsiness as a writer and share with the readers concerns and wishes. It is the obsession to learn new ways of responding, through our actions, to those challenges that we set in life what gives this handful of ideas a purpose and meaning.

In my courses, I have always remarked we cannot always choose what sorts of things happen to us. Sorrow and unexpectedness enjoy making a presence.
However, human beings can prepare to know what to do when something unexpected happens. That is our great responsibility. **Responsibility**, ability to respond.

Surely, we can live on without taking responsibilities. But, in my opinion, that way of living drives us to mediocrity and dejection, generating sorrow and anguish among ourselves and those around us. Once we have chosen to live a life of dejection and anguish, once we have chosen to live beyond the ethical purposes of responsibility, we can no longer have as many choices.
The price of freedom, the ability to choose, is paid in terms of responsibility. An irresponsible person lives unconsciously, getting further and further away from the possibility of choosing to do what is truly desired. Thus, given human beings are what they do, this person resigns deciding who to be.

I seem to have learned, thanks to my studies in Economics as well as through my work with different Organizations, the business world has an enormous power to transform society and human practice.
Throughout history, the business world has determined the way in which men and women act. No other human institution is more promising than the business world to generate lasting changes.

The following chapters rise from the conjunction of these institutions. On one hand, my belief in the need of teaching the Ethics of Responsibility and Freedom; on the other, my conviction that the most fruitful incumbency domain is that of the business world.
Every piece of understanding, each idea arisen from such domain can, undoubtedly, be applied to one's private life and personal growth. And vice versa.

The tools and concepts from the Transformative Learning presented in this book are the strong, healthy roots from a tree that extends its branches over all our doing, delivering its fruits beyond job matters.

This book is a simple attempt from the Strategic Ming and Soul. While you read it, I invite you to imagine life not as a succession of duties to be completed, but as a permanent path of commitment to Responsibility, Freedom, and Beauty.

**Starting Point**

The following ideas originate, but have been mutating since, from my experience as a college professor. With them, I try to build bridges between the realm of academia and the business world. I have always believed the assumed dichotomy between theory and practice to be wrong.

From the beginning, I noticed that, in order to understand business dynamics, Economics studies did not provide me with all the necessary conceptual tools. The answers I was capable of articulating in response to each of my questions were always incomplete. Searching for more practical ways to understand the economic and entrepreneurial phenomenon, I disembarked in Philosophy.

Naturally, what I thought to be the finish line rapidly turned into a fork multiplying the path into different lanes. Ontology of Language, Systems Thinking, Organizational Learning, Ethics of Responsibility and Freedom, Theory of Chaos and Systems Dynamics offer rough paths to begin the race.

Therefore, exploring these paths is the purpose of this book. Some of the paths we walk are rocky; others are smooth and flat, but always mysterious. And it is precisely this hidden characteristic what makes them unpredictable. It always is the uncertainty what makes us fall in love.

Navigating through these pages, the reader might find more questions than answers; more dead-ends than finish lines. In any case, I believe our mission of travelling together will be accomplished. Nobody returns home the same person once an adventure is over. That who leaves is not the same as that who comes back; this is what makes the trip worthy.

**Bases of Organizational Learning**

Every action responds to a theory. The most forceful practices are children to the most elevated abstract conceptions. Keynes used to say, "There is nothing more practical than a good theoretical disquisition." This is one of the few claims he made I agree with.
Logic bases that give it its conceptual context sustain an action theory. Without these pillars, actions are not effective and people cannot understand them.
In the field of human actions, the theory of Learning Organizations rises from a theoretical construction that recognizes, in my opinion, the input from a series of varied disciplines.
The confluence and synthesis in these disciplines provide the theoretical context where we start of our exploration.

In the first place, from Ontology of Language, I have taken the idea that human beings are linguistic beings, who live in conversations within a discursive drift. Everything we do happens within our language. And, given that our doing generates our becoming, that our being originates in our doing, our language is the context, the address of our being.
We are what we do, and when we change our actions, we change who we are. From this crucial philosophical understanding, Ontology of Language has let me incorporate, in practical form, conceptual tools that apply to numerous situations in private and work life.
Walking these paths, I could notice that Systems Thinking belongs to a branch from the same tree. The intuitions that emerge from the structural thinking systemic discipline proposes potentiate intuitions born from the Philosophy of Langujage. While Systems Thinking lets us see structures and interrelations, some tools provided by the Philosophy of Language, added to the science of Management, allow the

practice of Professional Coaching, making possible to efficiently intervene in such structures.

Remembering the whole, we start to become conscious about the way our actions impact on a reality that is much bigger than we usually notice at first sight. Ethics of Responsibility and Freedom helps us, in great measure, to live life to its fullest, occupying a place in the world where we develop our entire potential, assuming responsibility of the positive or negative consequences of our own actions.

Talking about freedom, in the modern Theory of Chaos I discovered an extremely promising theoretical base to solve the existing tension between creativity and order.
Systems Dynamics lets incorporating structural thinking tools to construct a graphic language, more adequate to understand the complexity of the phenomena in which the participating variables influence each other.

On the epistemological plane, Knowledge Biology's input becomes fundamental. This vision predisposes in a very adequate way to venture into the multiple postulates and tools of Organizational Learning.
Always within Epistemology, I found in Ayn Rand's Objectivism the philosophical scaffolding that concluded structuring my primitive ideas about freedom and leadership in life. Nowadays, I cannot conceive executive coaching, leadership and professional consulting without the decisive input from Rand's philosophy.

The conjunction of all these theories and practices, in addition to the learning life itself provides (such as the way I was raised, the things I saw and did, my loves and my passions) lead to the Executive Coaching technique I develop in my work life; technique I have named ConVersar—Getting Acquainted; technique whose virtues and failures I completely embrace, and that now I propose sharing its bases and applications.

**The Pillars**

Based on the established theoretical bases, the Transformative Learning Coaching ConVersar proposes depends on the development of personal competences that, taken into an organization, should build its foundational pillars. These abilities are:

a) A set of conversational practices oriented to effective actions
b) A way of operating sustained by shared values
c) System conception and Structural Thinking

a) Conversations in a Learning Organization

Talking seems to be a simple matter. It is an ability that, apparently, we all manage very well.

However, when it comes to talking about sensitive and complex topics, where commitment with the generation of actions needs to be clear, a great variety of difficulties arise. Almost all of us have experienced anguish and disappointment after having conversations in which, no matter how much we talk, we cannot accomplish a commitment whatsoever; we cannot make "things" happen.

People that compose a learning organization develop a set of practices that make it possible to take care of this difficulty, achieving individuals to improve, in great measure, their capacity to treat transcending issues, with a clear orientation to generate commitment with effective actions.

Generally speaking, we discover complex situations require more intelligence than that of a singular individual. The problem is that, when facing these kinds of situations, teams generally show behaviors characterized by the rigidity of the different taken positions, the defense of a point of view and the attack to all of those who do not share it.

The practice of Dialogue is the right tool to achieve improvements in the terrain of conversation development, increasing the capacity of listening to others, and favoring teamwork due to a better interpersonal communication.

This discipline's focal point is based on conversations oriented to effective actions and the incorporation of a culture sustained by shared values. That is, on two of the three mentioned pillars that constitutes the sustenance of learning organizations.

Dialogue is much more than a technique to help people talk. Actually, the idea that motivates this kind of conversation is to achieve new ways to coordinate actions within the organization, while modifying the mental models we use to design those actions in the first place. It does not look for agreement, but commitment and shared vision that lead to alignment.

b) Shared values

In order to accomplish that people who comprise an organization accept the challenge of continuous learning, fundamental requirement for Executiv Coaching to lead to a rise in productivity, is crucial they stop feeling threatened by the possible consequences of they ignorance.

In every learning process there is a period during which an individual does not have the necessary competences to take care of new practices. In such circumstances, the relationships between the people who form the organization need to rely on five fundamental values:

- Absolute **respect** for all people
- **Comprehension** that people always act according to their mental models
- **Humbleness** to accept that such mental models are merely a partial vision of a infinite reality
- A constant acceptance of new possibilities that let live life with **aspiration**

- The Ethics of **Freedom and Responsibility** as an irrevocable attitude of commitment to one's life and to assuming responsibility of one's actions

c) System Conception

When starting a group project, human beings face a series of barriers that many times undermine our chances to succeed. Said barriers tend to show as:
- An exaggerated fragmentation that leads us to think only in analytic terms; that is, focusing on the parts that constitute the phenomenon to explore
- The understanding of competence as the maximization of one's position over the shared interests of the team
- The tendency to act in a reactive form; that is, reacting to events instead of identifying and acting on structural causes

System thinking turns to be a very successful paradigm to develop a different vision, where **preeminence of the whole, cooperation**, and acting in a **generative** from, are the keys that open new paths of possibilities.

When analyzing a problem or exploring a particular situation, we develop an explanation of the phenomenon we are looking at. This explanation turns into the Mental Model of the situation, model we later on use to mentally simulate the possible results of the actions we imagine taking.

Our intuition is a great aid in such cases, but contains the inconvenient feature that it is not easily transferred to other individuals within the organization. This happens to be one of the main reasons for the lack of effective delegation in work groups.

The concepts and tools emerged from System Thinking and System Dynamics attempt to present the answer for this challenge. Through this methodology, it is possible to capture the various Mental Models, turn them into system causality diagrams to use them to imagine different courses of action.

These three pillars promote the possibility to attend the topics that allow daily, greater productivity operations. At the same time, I believe these practices build an alternative for personal growth for each of the individuals that participate in these activities.

**Two Paths Leading Towards Learning**

My friend Rubén Rolando, who has got a vast experience conducting learning and management development processes at IBM Latin America, points out that, not so long ago, the learnt abilities during school or college, usually midst the individual's youth, used to let each of us face most of the challenges throughout our lifetime.

Rubén notices the present is quite different, although. Today, it is necessary to develop new abilities in a permanent form if we want to keep, not only efficiency in our actions, but also harmony in our lives.

In this context, people need to rethink their interests and objectives if they truly want to take care of a dynamic world. Then, we need to concern about a matter of great importance: to define what is the attitude to adopt when facing this challenge. Thereby, I identify two possible courses of action:

1) To acquire the flexibility that lets us adapt quickly to change (if possible to be the first to do so) or,
2) To lead the change

In both cases, the need to learn new practices and abilities is clear. The first possibility deals with learning to detect what are the new circumstances, identifying how are we disturbing the harmony of those new circumstances, and developing a new behavior that amends the situation. This process is called *Error Correction and Detection*.

The second course is, in my opinion, more powerful, as it aims towards a deeper intervention. It implies what I like to call *Learn to Learn*.

Whatever path is chosen, it will be necessary to go through a continuous learning process, during which the competences and abilities needed to progress in "chaos" ought to be acquired.

Peter Senge clearly poses the necessity to develop systems capable of constant learning, observing what are the recurrent practices and reflecting about them in order to make them better for organizations, in his book, *The Fifth Discipline*.
Arie de Geus, one of the precursors for the concept of Learning Organizations, claims, *"The only competitive advantage sustained in time is the organization's capacity for constant learning."*
While interpreting the discipline *Learn to Learn* as a personal competence, I manifest my conviction that it is thanks to **people** development we accomplish more productive entrepreneurial organizations.

### Executive Coaching and the nature of Managerial Work

More than once I have had the chance to talk with my friend Roberto Ayling, Marsh Inc. Managing Director, about the nature of managerial work. I must admit my role during these conversations is exclusively limited to listening to what Roberto explains. It is the best way for me to take advantage of his great wisdom.

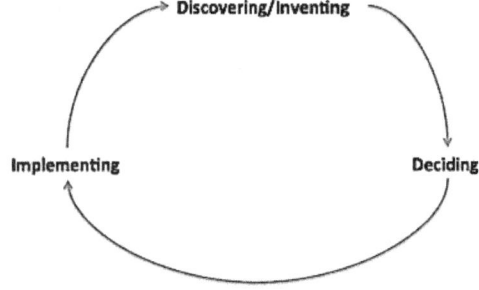

This is how I have been able to understand that the task people responsible of directing entrepreneurial organizations can be synthesized in three fundamental steps. Each step refers to the following, and together they form a constant feedback circle.
The first step is about **Discovering** opportunities, problems or threats before competitors on the market. This implies seeing what is new, what is yet to be organized, what is hidden, or, best-case scenario, what is merely suggested within surrounding conditions.

In this context, discovering resembles to **Inventing**. It is about making new articulations to interpret the world. Someone who makes an invention creates a new interpretation of the facts that constitute the external reality. If well founded, this interpretation opens new paths of possibilities.
This takes us to the second step, the moment of **Deciding**. When new action possibilities arise, managers or executives need to choose among the possible solutions, discarding others, while trying to design the most creative and profitable courses of action. The thinking structures that influence their choices determine their management's success. Further on, we will see this deals with more complex elections, where the tension between the short and the long run, between productivity and integrity manifests itself.

The third step is **Implementing**. Decisions are worth little or nothing if they do not translate to effective actions. When implementing, we try to place in the real world what still belongs to the ideas world. It is the supreme moment for commitment with effective actions.
Of course, the implementation process it is not just the Managerial Work loop's final stage. It is also the beginning of a new loop for learning and decision-making. Just like implementation leads to results, it will also be the instant in which we compare what we obtained with what we looked for. The gap between these two must become the source of new exploration and reflection, leading to a new stage of discovering and inventing.

On the next pages, I intend to explain a set of conceptual tools and effective practices that I believe are greatly auspicious to improve the Managerial Work loop.

Regarding the stage of Discovering or Inventing, we will explore the disciplines of Mental Models, the Inference Ladder, Learn to Learn, Productive Questioning and Structural Thinking.

To improve the quality of our Decisions, we will look into the practice of Dialogue, the Art of Speaking Truthfully, Team Learning, and Context and Confirmation Techniques; while revaluing the Ethics of Responsibility and Freedom.

Finally, we will see that if we incorporate the abilities and possibilities given by Commitment Management, building Trust, Managing the unexpected and Emotional Intelligence and Ability, the Implementation step ends up being more effective.

Each of these disciplines and practices aim to impact over four intervention and action results measurement spaces: the company's **Economic Results** (do they allow the generation of wealth?), the domain of Technical Skills (do they improve efficiency?) the space fo **Interpersonal Relationships** (do they improve team work and action coordination quality?), and the area of **Individual Development** (do they propitiate emotional balance and individual performance satisfaction?). This method arises under the impression that is individual growth and its application to improve human interaction what should propitiate the permanent optimization of economic results.

**A digression on Intelligence**

At this point, I think it is necessary to explain my own idea of what "intelligence" is. Far from considering it a "gift", a "biological" condition "printed" in our DNA, I believe intelligence is an ability. The ability to recognize different characteristics a situation or phenomenon presents, added to the capacity of putting those distinctions in order to obtain the achievements proposed, while respecting the values composing the life ethics we wish to honor.

I confess I have arrived to this "definition" (if I am even allowed to call it so) of intelligence after several years of debating with colleagues and, mostly, students in my classes or participants in my workshops.

Given my understanding of management is based on three important competences (Thinking, Communicating, Managing Emotions) the "matter of intelligence" raises as a question or food for thought.

While treating the first of these managerial competences (Thinking) is almost impossible to avoid raising the question: what is intelligence?

This is how, trying different answers for this recurring question, I could arrive to this categorization of "intelligence" that presents the following characteristics.

1- Intelligence is a kind of ABILITY. As such, it is not different than speaking a foreign language, cooking steak or throwing a ball. Abilities are composed by actions. We say we "have" ability when we are capable of realizing such actions, according to the quality bar we have set.

As any other ability, intelligence can be learnt and improved. Human beings are not born "having" certain ability. In any case, our DNA possesses information making it easier to develop the ability. Genetic information proposes, but does not guarantee.

In order to tame certain ability (signing, dancing, playing football or exercising intelligence), it is necessary to learn and train the actions composing it.

2- Distinguishing, which is noticing different characteristics in a situation or phenomenon, is the first action composing the ability of intelligence. In order to become capable of interfering in a given situation, it is indispensable to see the qualities it possesses (different components, colors, materials, dynamics, etc.). Whoever finds it impossible to distinguish, becomes "lost" in the situation, without any chance to notice different alternatives of actions.

3- The capacity of distinguishing is always referred to a certain domain of action. When we talk about the ability of intelligence, it is always bound to a specific domain. Nobody "is" fully intelligent, but you are always intelligent (ability) within the limits of a peculiar context.

4- In order for "intelligence" to be complete, it is not enough to only have the "theory". Intelligence is linked to action. It must make us able to "do" something. Therefore, together with the capacity of distinguishing, it is crucial that such ability becomes useful to accomplish the results we have proposed. Intelligence implies achieving results. Results DO matter. We cannot call ourselves intelligent beings in a certain domain if we are not capable of obtaining the results we had set in the beginning.

5- It is important to notice we are talking about "results WE have set". Intelligence is more than just chasing objectives. It implies the capacity of inventing such objectives, of self-imposing the search of those results. Even when the objectives are set by other people (a CEO, for example), when the intelligent subject decides to accept them, he or she is making them his/her own. Then, intelligence involves the ability of appropriating other people's goals.

6- Finally, intelligence is composed by values. Every intelligent person has a set of values that constitutes his/her Moral. The moral is conformed by a "list" of values the person has chosen to look after. While we call "moral" to that "list of values", we call Ethics the way that person deals with those values, "intertwines" them in a certain way, making them their actions guide.

The "moral" is a set of values; the "ethics" is a reasoning logic. Intelligence needs both the moral and ethics. If one, or both, of them are missing, we will only achieve "cunning". We might say cunning is intelligence stripped of values.

**Setting sail**

Perhaps, the reader might note there is in this book a feeling that life itself is an apprenticeship. I sincerely hope that is the main message engaged by my efforts in writing this book. I am absolutely convinced we need to generate the attitude and the skills of an apprentice. We need to develop a state of curiosity and surprise, of respect for mystery, of a careful exploration and of love for questions.

This is not an easy task. End results are not guaranteed either. It will be the commitment with which we take on the task, you and I, what will make the attempt not be in vain. We will need courage. Or just like I like to say, alluding to the fútbol (soccer) language I learnt during my childhood, we will need "heart and short passes". Strategic Mind and Soul. Emotions and Conscience. Two sides of the same coin.

No one ever comes back from a trip. When we leave the port, we abandon objects, people, places, but we also abandon that person we were before departing, forever. When we come back, the port will neither be the same.
My esteemed reader, in you I farewell that person who embarks on this trip. We both know that, if this adventure is worth it, we will not see it again.

# Chapter 1
## Apprentices and Know-it-alls

-"Let's make a sacred pact. I promise to teach karate and do my part. You promise to learn what I say you do, and do your part."

With this simple and direct proposition, Mister Miyagi showed Daniel Larusso how their relationship would develop, if he truly intended to become an apprentice in the attempt to master the techniques of Karate.

*Karate Kid* is a film produced in 1984 that tells the story of Mr. Miyagi, a peculiar martial arts professor, and his only student, Daniel, a teenager that just moved to San Fernando Valley, near Los Angeles.
Aside from the combats, young love and the Hollywood ending, throughout the film it is possible to notice the huge difference that exists between two totally opposed learning paradigms: Apprentice or know-it-all.
The film shows the transformation happening in Daniel. At first, he believes to know karate; that is what he tells Miyagi when they first meet.
However, Daniel does not really know karate. Even worse, he does not know karate, and he does not know he does not know. Under this circumstance, his chances to learn karate are null. Thinking he knows, his ego is safe. He is a total know-it-all, with quick answers to every question in the field of self-defense.
Only an external factor, usually negative, and may be even brutal, can get a know-it-all out of his blindness. Like we said, Daniel's ego remains safe, but not his body.
One night, Daniel painfully learns he does not really know karate. On that night, Daniel gets beat up by a group of teenagers from his high school.

Defeated, in pain and confused, Daniel seeks for help, and finds in in Miyagi. He acknowledges he does not know and asks to teach him karate. Humility (it is not strange nor coincidental that humility comes from the same root as humiliation) has turned him into an apprentice.

I believe this is a very powerful transformation. The practices, actions and, mainly, results that comprise these two visions are diametrically opposed. Without jumping into any conclusions, it is worth exploring a little further into this first learning issue.

Then, the first thing we can do is to make it clear there are two basic postures towards the challenges something new proposes, what we do not know but wish to learn.

To illustrate this matter, we can look at an example from my days travelling the world, visiting multiple cities, in many different countries.

This story in particular happened in Córdoba, Argentina, a place I love, where some of my beloved friends live.

There I was, taking the lead in one of my Workshops about Leadership and, like it usually happens, someone asked a question. When I began my answer, I replied:

-"It is totally understandable it seems a little strange and unconventional to you. As an apprentice, there still are some aspects about leadership you struggle to comprehend".

However, something happening on the other side of the room immediately caught my attention; a woman raising her hand just about I started speaking, long before I finished my explanation. Even though we need to be cautious when interpreting other people's gestures, I was quite sure she seemed a little upset about something I had said.

Anyways, I continued with what I was doing and, once I was over, I asked her what was her question.

In a state of mind I interpreted to be empowered by daze (perhaps the fact that I kept talking instead of paying immediate attention to her raised hand made it worse), the lady asked me:

-"And why did you downgrade her like that?"

I have to admit she caught me by surprise. I did not understand what she was referring to. Of course, I asked her to clarify whom had I "downgraded" and in what way.

-"Well, that lady that just asked you that question! Why did you need to downgrade her by treating her as an *apprentice*?"

I believe the anecdote is quite eloquent. In that lady's mental model, apprentice is connected with not knowing, with ignorance. And, of course, in said mental model, "ignorant" is an insult, a disqualifying adjective.

That is, precisely, the mental model I call the "Know-it-all's Paradigm".

The know-it-all is someone who tries to be right all the time. Someone that cannot stand not knowing. For a know-it-all, ignorance, which is the absence of immediate answers to a question, is a degrading experience.

Some people take this mental model to an extreme. Their only concern is to "look good", to not show themselves ignorant. In such case, they would rather hide their ignorance and, therefore, forgo their effectiveness by stopping to ask the questions that would unveil their lack of knowledge. The know-it-all ends have only having ears for their ego's desperate call: *"Look good, at any price. Do not let anyone know of your incompetence."*

In the know-it-all's mental model, ego ends up becoming a tyrannical master.

Fortunately, there is one other possibility, a completely different paradigm, the Apprentice's Mental Model. This is someone totally different from the know-it-all. The apprentice does not always tries to be right all the time, nor boasts about everything he knows, but is proud of everything he is capable of learning. An apprentice is not committed to satisfying his ego, but reaching effectiveness in his actions. The apprentice does not aim to look good, but to achieve results. In any case, this is what satisfies his ego (which, of course, is also present): attaining positive results, reaching his objectives.

I would like to clarify I am convinced that most of our educational tradition is oriented to knowing rather than learning. My personal experience tells me that reward and punishment systems, social acceptance, tend to celebrate the end product of knowing, instead of acknowledging merits throughout the learning process.
Hardly ever one receives an award for asking a question. It is much more common to be acclaimed for a quick answer. And, many times, without even caring too much about its precision.

The paradigm of knowing it all, then, sets us a trap. Overpowered by the need of looking "wise", we end up missing the chance to learn.
In order to get around this "trap of knowing", we will need to dig deeper in the apprentice's way.
Lets try to answer a decisive question: How can we learn to learn?

**Learning to Learn**

Learning always means to leave behind (at least momentarily) places, practices and customs familiar to us. One never learns if not willing to walk new paths, to change certainties for uncertainties, to replace old skills for new competences.
On a first level, a quite primary one, human beings do not need an explanation of how to learn. After all, since our lives' very beginning we embark on that hard task we call learning. Walking and talking are two examples of skills we learn in an autonomous way, without any teachers that explain us any theory.
But, this same learning skill, supposedly innate, ends up taking us to develop a basic incompetence. Towards the false certainty we know what is necessary to do in order to learn, we focus our attention on WHAT and HOW MUCH to learn, instead to checking HOW to learn. Nonetheless, the skill we might acquire to learn tremendously impacts on the quality of our relationships with other people, on our work's effectiveness and, generally, on our wellbeing.

There is an inevitable starting point on the learning path. It starts with commitment, with an unbreakable decision of walking through each of the trails, curves and nooks, always mysterious, that an apprentice faces.

We encounter then, the first challenge on the learning path:

1- Constructing a vision

It is commonly said someone who does not know where he is going cannot get lost. Of course, he cannot arrive either. The process of constructing a vision is fundamental to reach learning. One needs to identify the place one wants to get to. Without a vision, it is impossible to advance. Like Ayn Rand states: "Throughout the centuries there were men who took first steps down new roads armed with nothing but their own vision."

Sadly enough, many apprentice's aspirants fail in this first step. Since they consider it a trivial matter, they rush to take ulterior steps, making them fail over and over again in their attempt to acquire new competences. This way, tired, ashamed and with a broken self-esteem, they give up. They end up being defeated by the enemies of learning.

Having a vision has a strategic value. It lets us set evaluation criteria. If we do not clearly know where we are headed, it will be impossible to determine if we are better or worse off, if we have moved forwards or backwards. It will be impossible to establish rationality criteria for our actions if we do not set an objective beforehand.

When the apprentice succeeds in constructing a vision, everything starts to look clearer. Of course, there still is a long way ahead. Actually, this is the point where we start to see the path, full with its roughness, mysteries and challenges. At least, now we have somewhere to get to, and a road that takes us there.

When I was barely five years old, my parents took me to see a classic film revival: *The Wizard of Oz*.
There is a scene in the film that shows the importance of having a vision. Dorothy is lost, not knowing where to go or what path to take. Then, she finds the Good Witch of the East, who helps her explore what is in her heart, what is her greatest desire. It is then when Dorothy understands what she really wants is to get back home. "There is no place like home", Dorothy says. As soon as she says this, a long, yellow path appears ahead. This road leads to Emerald City, where the Great Wizard of Oz lives, the only person able to help Dorothy return home, in Arkansas.
There will still be a long way to walk, lots of dangers to overcome and many fellow travellers to recruit. But, the path, meandering and inviting, promising and mysterious, already extends ahead. And she will get back home.

Learning is always a force that comes from within. Only then we will have the energy needed to overcome different challenges. It must be something we really want to achieve, something we desire intensely.
Sometimes, we try to learn something just to please others, or to look better to other people. That way, the force we call from within is inspired in an external source. Inevitably, and rather sooner than later, we end up exhausting our forces, since we are not attending to our most personal purposes. Learning to "look good" is one of the know-it-all greatest weaknesses.

Only a true apprentice will be able to generate a vision that moves him. Then, like in the movie, a long way will extend ahead. It will be the moment to take the second step:

2- Making an Incompetence Statement / Avowal

Establishing a vision is just the first step, essential, but only the first.
One more time, the mental models of an apprentice or a know-it-all become relevant.

Acknowledging there is a gap is accepting there is something missing, something we do not have yet, something is lacking. It is, then, to concede we do not know.
This task is particularly impossible for a know-it-all. His affection towards quick answers prevents him from asking open questions. It keeps him from acknowledging he does not know. It is important to clarify that I am not passing judgment on this kind of attitude; I am just trying to describe it. I am noting an action or, more precisely, the lack of one. In short, a know-it- all does NOT accept his ignorance.

This reflection on the know-it-all's attitude takes us back to a matter we had begun to explore and left behind, but only for a little while: the nature of ignorance.
We had said many people think "ignorant" is an insult (Do you remember the lady in Córdoba that questioned me for calling someone else an "apprentice"?)
I am convinced this opinion about ignorance or ignorant has comes from another mental model: the mental model of Knowledge.

As we have said, we live in a society that rewards the know-it-all. Our culture acclaims those who give (if possible, quick) answers to every question. Answers grant acknowledgement, economic wealth, power and self-esteem, while ignorance generates contempt, rejection and shame.
I ought to clarify I am not stating answers are not important. Of course they are. What I intend to express is they are not the ONLY important resource.
Naturally, if we find someone who gives effective answers for our questions, this will help our own effectiveness. There are many people that have a vast quantity of answers for questions in CERTAIN ACTION DOMAINS. However, there are no people who have effective answers for EVERY question. That is, exactly, what a know-it-all pretends and wishes, which ends up leading him to deceit and self-deceit.
Just having questions and never attempting to find their answers is as ineffective as running away from them, and blocking them to stick with the already known answers.

The former acts as a kind of "bar talk", vain and without any commitment with actions; the latter, inhibits learning and prevents innovation.

But lets go back to the mental model of knowledge, which is, in my opinion, the root of this matter.
Firstly, I am certain the dichotomy between ignorance and wisdom is FALSE. Even further, it is not only false. It is extremely dangerous.

Wise and ignorant are not opposites, but different stations of the same trip. In order to get to wisdom, the apprentice must begin by admitting his ignorance. He will not truly be an apprentice if he cannot make this statement.
The learning process is sponsored by the discovery of dissatisfaction. There is something lacking, something not working as someone desires. This is a situation this person cannot modify, given his current competences. Learning requires a lot of effort. This effort is justified by the acquisition of such competences, the ones that ought to change this unpleasant reality.

When we modify the relation between ignorance and wisdom, when we stop seeing them as opposites and start understanding them as different stages towards a common goal, we start to construct a model of knowledge that makes learning easier.
This model allows distinguishing three different spaces. Said spaces appear as a consequence of three different statements, but closely related.

1. I know that I know
2. I know that I do not know
3. I do not know that I do not know

Lets explore each of these.

<u>I know that I know</u>: One who states he knows, also states he is conscious of such wisdom. He knows he can produce effective actions in that domain of action.

He knows he finds himself in his WISDOM space.

I know that I do not know: When we state we do not know, what we are also saying is WE KNOW WE DO NOT KNOW. We express we are conscious about the absence of knowledge. We acknowledge we find ourselves in our space of ignorance. The interesting part, beautiful part, of this is that when we look at it this way, we are aware the statement of ignorance begins conjugating the verb to know. I state that I KNOW that I do not know. Ignorance becomes a very subtle type of wisdom.

I do not know that I do not know: This statement is somewhat paradoxical. It implies that I am not even conscious of my own ignorance. Out lack of competence is such that we do not even know it exists. We find ourselves in our space of BLINDNESS. I describe it as paradoxical since it is a statement we do not state. Exactly for that reason is why we are blind. We do not know that we do not know, and we cannot state it. The doors for learning seem closed and it does not look like there is a chance to open them.

As we can see on the figure above, the spaces for wisdom and ignorance are closed circles, while blindness is open to infinity.

I was saying the space for blindness is paradoxical, give that when we state our own blindness, we immediately move on to the space of ignorance. When we acknowledge, "I do not know that I do not know", we become conscious of that lack of wisdom and we ALREADY BELONG to the space of ignorance. Thus, I argued this one is an "impossible statement". Its own mention vanishes it.

In order to move from ignorance to wisdom, we need answers. In order to move from blindness to ignorance, new questions. Finally, we have what I consider to be the greatest comprehension shift this model generates: We do not get to wisdom if not through ignorance. In order to be wiser, first, we need to ask new questions. So, TO BECOME WISER, FIRST, WE NEED TO BECOME MORE IGNORANT.

When an apprentice has incorporated this comprehension, he has defeated a great enemy, a mortal trap: the trap of the know-it-all.

Then, he is ready for the third step.

### 3- Accepting the gap between vision and current reality

In order to learn, it is essential for the apprentice to acknowledge the existing gap between his vision, which is the capacity level he wants to achieve, and his current competence.

This gap works as the learning engine. It generates what we call "creative tension".

The following drawing helps us understand this concept.

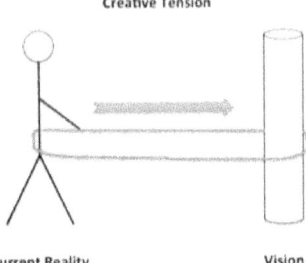

The vision is represented by a stake, in the future. It has to be far enough so the apprentice does not think he will get to it with minimum effort.
However, it is crucial there is a connection between him and his vision. On the drawing, such connection is represented by an elastic tape that joins the apprentice with the vision.
The tape must always be tense, so it encourages the apprentice to move forward.
If there is no tension, which Peter Senge called "Creative Tension", there will be no movement. But, if the vision is totally disconnected from the apprentice's current reality, he will not be able to note the relation between his current competence and his goal, which will probably make him abandon the task.

The movie *Rocky* represents a good example of a connection between current reality and personal vision. Again, a film is useful to illustrate what I am trying to show. It should not be strange, since the cinema is art. And art, is always a source for inspiration and, at the same time, an exaltation of the good and bad, beautiful and grotesque, in our lives.
Might be an unnecessary clarification, but *Rocky* is a United Artist film, starred and written by Sylvester Stallone, which won The Academy Award for Best Film in 1976. It tells the story of an unknown, low-class boxer, who is chosen to fight Apollo Creed, the undisputed Heavyweight Champion of the

World, as part of the United States Declaration of Independence Bicentennial celebrations.
The night before the fight, Rocky cannot sleep well. He has trained too hard and his whole life's greatest challenge is only a few hours away. Uneasy, he walks out of bed and goes to the stadium, an empty and silent giant, waiting to be filled with emotions and excitement hours ahead. Rocky walks through it, while he observes two big curtains showing his and Apollo's figures. At that moment, in the middle of the sleeping and longing stadium, he realizes he will not be able to beat Apollo. He understands Creed's skills will make him unbeatable. Then, he generates a vision, he makes a commitment with himself.
He gets back home, where Adrian, his wife, asks him what was going on. Rocky tells her:
-"I can't beat him. Adrian, it's true. I was nobody. But that don't matter either, you know? 'Cause I was thinkin', it really don't matter if I lose this fight. It really don't matter if this guy opens my head, either. 'Cause all I wanna do is go the distance. Nobody's ever gone the distance with Creed, and if I can go that distance, you see, and that bell rings and I'm still standin', I'm gonna know for the first time in my life, see, that I weren't just another bum from the neighborhood."

Rocky does not generate a vision in which he either wins the fight or the title. His goal is not as far-fetched, but connected to his possibilities. He will there, standing, taking hits and holding on when the bell rings for the last time, at the end of the fifteenth round for the greatest Title in the world.

Then, the creative tension is the engine that pushes us towards the goal. But, is there any force that makes it harder to achieve our goal?
Just like we can represent our vision by a stake in the future, which makes us go towards it, there also are negative forces that make our way more difficult.
In order to complete our drawing, we can say there also is a stake placed on our back, which prevents us from moving forward.

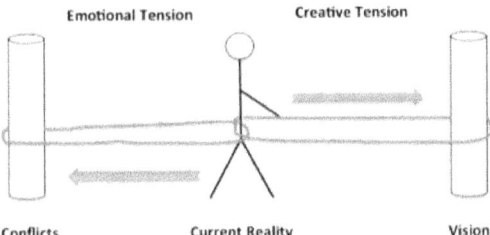

On one side we can see the creative tension, which connects our current reality with the vision we have formulated. On the other side, we all have a set of unsolved conflicts that prevent us from moving forward.

Generally, these conflicts are explanations of past facts, loaded with negative opinions about our competences and our possibilities to learn or change behaviors.

While the creative tension pushes us forward, the emotional tension pulls us backwards. And there we are, standing still before our incapacity to solve the dynamics provoked by these two tensions.

How do we solve this dilemma? There is always a great temptation, which consists of degrading our vision. When we make our vision smaller, we have the illusion that our goal is closer (in *Rocky*'s case, he would be happy to reach the fifth round, for example). But, what we are actually doing is renouncing to greatness, to our most desired dreams.

If asked, we will say we have chosen to pursue a "more realistic" vision. This way, we justify our actions before other people, as much as ourselves.

But that is, exactly, the great renunciation to which we are tempted. Our personal vision does not need to be "realistic"; it just needs to be connected with our current reality. But, I insist, it needs to be as far away as possible. It will be that greatest distance what will generate the necessary creative tension to learn. Degrading our vision diminishes the creative tension, but it only works for so long.

Acting this way, we are actually sticking the stake on our back deeper into the ground, because no matter how hard we try, we will never cheat ourselves. When we diminish the greatness of our objectives, all we are doing is feeding the list of opinions about or own weakness, generating an increasing emotional tension.

If the apprentice tries to move forward, the dynamics generated between these tensions will put him in a trap he will not escape, if he does not solve the emotional tension first; that is, attempting to ignore the structural conflicts formed by his own personal negative opinions.
Moving forward, towards the Personal Vision, the "elastic tape" on the right loses some tension, since the apprentice at least a step closer. Meanwhile, stepping a step away from the stake of explanations about own weakness, the tension on the left (emotional tension) will increase.
The system will not be at rest, given emotional tension overcomes creative tension. The next step will mostly likely be towards the direction in which maximum tension is resolved. That is, a step backwards. Along with that step, the apprentice will reaffirm his opinions about his own weakness, stopping to see them as opinions, in order to start taking them as inflexible facts about his "personality".
This is why I call this phenomenon the "immense strength of our weaknesses".

To resolve the emotional tension, the apprentice must be capable of understanding that the opinions about his weaknesses come from past experiences, during which his actions were not effective and he was not competent enough to meet the proposed checkpoints on that opportunity.
But, not being capable of doing something in the past does not condemn him to never being capable in the future. It is the moving strength that learning has what lets him be competent the next time.

Only when the apprentice understands that his explanations about his own weakness are actually opinions (which are subject to change), he will be able to see the learning gap as something possible to walk through and will be able to notice which actions will get him near to his vision.

Those actions he still cannot perform are precisely the ones that belong to the domain of learning he is willing to walk through.

Lets go back to our *Karate Kid* example. Daniel has painfully discovered he does NOT know karate. He has been brutally beat up and threatened to suffer future beatings. But, in the middle of the night, when he was being smacked, one person came to his aid, and, with great ease, he thwarted his aggressors. That person was Mister Miyagi. From then on, Daniel places himself in his hands to guide him through the rough path that entails learning self-defense.

Then, we get to the fourth step of learning:

4- Finding a Master and ask for help

It is the time to ask for help. Once again, only an apprentice is capable of asking help. The know-it-all, even though he might have acknowledged his incompetence in what would be a very unlikely situation, will try to hide it from everyone else. His ego will demand him to exhaust all possibilities in order to "look good". In a know-it-all's mental model, seeking for help does not "look good".

On the other hand, the apprentice wishes to fix his incompetence, so he seeks a master, he asks for help. As we said at the beginning of the chapter, they make a deal: the master teaches, the apprentice learns.

One more time, *Karate Kid* is a useful example. Once the learning pact is sealed, Miyagi asks Daniel to polish his car, wax his floors, and to paint a fence. Despite Daniel's skepticism towards these tasks, he performs them. He has asked for help, sealed a pact, so he plays his part.

Work is hard and, at first, does not seem to be fruitful. Daniel is not doing what he thought a karate-like training would be. Here we find another crucial characteristic in the process of learning: The apprentice, as long as he is an apprentice, by definition, he DOES NOT KNOW. Hence, he CANNOT SEE what seems obvious to the master.
At this time, the apprentice needs complete trust on his master. If there is a break, if the apprentice doubts in his master, and the master cannot uphold as such, the learning process will have failed.
In the movie, Daniel gets tired of polishing, waxing and painting. He does not understand why those tasks would be useful for his karate skills. He beings to doubt, so he wants to quit. Then, Miyagi shows Daniel what he could not see: asking to reproduce the movements from all those tasks, he shows him how much he has advanced with his karate competences. The master is upheld, and the apprentice definitely seals his commitment with the training. Henceforth, the path becomes clearer.

One of the critical steps in learning is the moment in which the apprentice, convinced of his incompetence, decides to ask for help.
The master, then, is constituted by the apprentice himself. Nobody is master on its own, but until the moment in which other person chooses him as such and asks for help.

A large portion of success in learning resides in the decision of identifying a master.

The relationship between the master and the apprentice shows three characteristics:
1. The student asking for help and constituting a master
2. The student giving the master the permission to judge his performance in such domain of action
3. The apprentice promising to complete the tasks and practices the master chooses, without questioning their validity or effectiveness.

These three characteristics imply that when choosing a person as his master, the student involves in the process the matters that concern personal autonomy, dignity and trust.
Autonomy and dignity is strongly related to authority. The student sees in his master someone capable of generating (in such domain) actions far more effective than his. This goes back to the definition of power we discussed in the introduction (capacity of generating effective actions in a specific domain of action).
Thus, as every type of power comes from some sort of authority, what we are saying is the student acknowledges his master's authority in that domain and submits to his power. This is why his autonomy and dignity are in play.

It is important we are careful with the meaning that verbs like "submit" and subjects like "autonomy" and "dignity" acquire. We are not dealing with a submission by force, externally imposed, but a free choice made by the apprentice.
This matter is clearly exposed, therefore resolved, when the apprentice understands he himself is the primary SOURCE OF AUTHORITY. Every power emerges from an Authority, and every authority originates from a Source of authority.
In the case of learning, the source of authority is the apprentice himself, his opinions about his master's ethics and competence, what generates the basic emotionality of the necessary Trust to walk through the learning path.
When the apprentice understands he gives his master the authority to teaching, he accepts to submit to the power that emerges from such authority. And, keeps to himself the right of taking away that authority if considers it so. In that case, the apprentice will cease to submit to his master's power. That is his right. The cost he will incur will be the impossibility to continue his learning. The student cannot take away the authority and, simultaneously, continuing the process with the same master. It is one thing or the other.

The leaning process is not "democratic". Rather, it relies on inequality. The master is NOT equal to the student. If this inequality is not accepted, them learning will not take place.

The times that I have faced this issue throughout my professional career! On different occasions, I have noticed people that attended my classes, seminars or conferences without intending to learn. Many times, they feel their bosses, their superiors on the hierarchical scale of their organization, have "made them go".
In such state of mind, people do not give me authority, so I lack the power to teach them. Their only objective when they participate is to demonstrate they already knew what I "pretend" to show them. It is like they were saying: "It is true, I am here. But, I did not need to be. And I am going to show it".
Clearly, in such circumstances, those people will barely learn anything. Learning is not compatible with arrogance.

Another curious, and equally ineffective, case happens when people admit their ignorance, but, even so, are not willing to give anyone else any authority. It is like they said: "Very well. I do not know. But if I do not know, then nobody else does".
In these cases, the alleged student tries to contradict every single instruction, example and action guide the master provides, acting as if he knew more and better.
Naturally, there is not much to do in this case either. Such person is a victim of a fatal contradiction. Either he admits he does not know and gives authority, or he already knows and does not need a master's aid. But he cannot have BOTH THINGS AT A TIME.

The relationship between the apprentice and the master is constructed upon asymmetry. Like every asymmetric relation, it risks falling on abuse. If this happens, the apprentice's dignity will be in stake.
To minimize this risk, the student needs to determine, in the first place and clearly, what are the limits of the domain in which he is asking for help and in which he admits authority and submits to the power of the chosen master.

Only if the matter of trust in the master, and dignity and autonomy of the student, has been properly resolved, then we can move on to the next step.

5- Making a learning commitment

Making a commitment underlies making a promise. In the case of the apprentice, it is about promising he will continue to move forward even when strength starts to weaken, when difficulties seem to be insurmountable and when paths become impenetrable. No matter how many obstacles block the way, nor difficulties to be faced, the apprentice will try by every means to continue his way towards the objective.

The strength of that commitment, which the apprentice makes with himself (not with someone else), will let the apprentice overcome, for example, the barriers generated from experiencing his own incompetence.
By necessity, the apprentice does not know. And, given that to learn his needs to practice, he will not be able to avoid, at the beginning, his actions being totally ineffective. Many times, this is the main cause for quitting the process: not being able to stand the "shame" of seeing himself (and other people seeing him) incompetent.
The end objective of every learning process is to increase competence in a domain of action. Thus, the apprentice ought to know if he is to succeed it is precisely because the effectiveness of his actions is LOWER than the one he will have when learning has taken place. Rather than being ashamed of his current levels of competence, the apprentice should focus on the pride that makes him capable of overcoming challenges and improving everything there is to improve. As we said earlier, his self-esteem should come from what he can learn, not from what he already knows.

In order to do this, it is highly important he is willing to leave behind old practices, even if these have been effective in the past. They are not effective for new demands and tasks (which the apprentice has freely accepted), so they need to be changed for new ones. But it is crucial the apprentice acknowledges that, to carry the same actions as people who know, first, he needs to learn to carry the actions people who do NOT know

(but they are learning). This understanding is decisive and determines if learning will happen or not.
The person that seeks to learn needs to see himself as a beginner and give himself permission to make mistakes. He should not try to "skip" stages. He should not pretend to "look good" from the beginning.

At all times, during his learning process, it is very useful the apprentice has clearly understood the different checkpoints throughout the learning path. On the road to competence, there are different moments. It is worth it to clarify them.
The first one we will call the **Beginner.**
As soon as someone states he has become an apprentice and starts to comply with the commitment this implies, he is set in beginner level. A good beginner knows he is not competent in such domain. But, he is less worried about his current looks than his future level of competence. All he does is to follow his master's instructions, without questioning or underestimating his suggestions. Many of his actions are limited to copying his masters'. His autonomy is almost non-existent. His master tells him what actions to carry or not. Rather than his master's guide, he cannot generate any effective action.
Further, all of his actions require his attention. He is totally incapable of carrying any automatic action within the domain in which he is being introduced.
To illustrate this, lets think about a piano student. When he is a beginner, all he can do is to look at his master and to imitate his movements.

After some time and lots of dedication, we arrive at the second station: **Competent Under Supervision.**
On this level, an important change starts to show. The apprentice begins to execute some of the effective actions in the new domain. The complex levels he can face are still very low, but some of the actions are now possible for him.
His autonomy is merely superior to a beginner's, since he only carries actions under his master's direct supervision. Nonetheless, his own experience begins to be an alternative

guide for action, and he can use it to draw conclusions and make some decisions.

He starts to automate some of his actions, without the need to permanently reflect about each of them.

In the case of our earlier example about the piano student, the competent under supervision has changed places. He no longer is standing behind his master watching how he plays the piano. Now, he plays the keys and the master observes and makes corrections. The student is now capable of playing simple scores somewhat fluently, but he cannot solve the challenges he might face. Every novelty paralyzes him and goes back to needing his master's direct guide.

The next level is **Competent.** Here, the student has developed a set of skills that allow him to operate adequately. The characteristic standing out on this level, compared to the two previous ones, is autonomy; given that the student now follows the rules his experience taught him. Further, the competent does not need to spend much time reflecting on the actions to carry, since he now makes them fluently and harmonically. He takes responsibility in breaks he might experience in such domain. Only great, unexpected difficulties will interrupt the flux of his actions, making him reflect. The competent generates RESULTS.

On this level, our piano student has become a pianist. He plays without interruptions or reflections on each score. Only the most complex ones will make him think how to carry on. When he plays Mozart, for example, anyone who is familiar with Mozart's work will be able to recognize it when they listen to our pianist.

Here, it would seem there are no more levels, that there is nothing else after being competent. But, there is. The next level is to become **Virtuous.**

The actions carried out by the virtuous almost completely lack deliberation. They are fluent, and he does not need to reflect on them while executing. To him, they are totally "transparent" actions. His competence level is such that these actions do not need his reflective attention. When a major break happens, the virtuous has a great quantity of tools at hand. Not only he mends the break, but also shows new ways to fix it. The virtuous sets new standards of action. He tries new ways to act in such domain. He executes all the imaginable actions and puts in them his personal, distinctive style.

He is the genius interpreter, the one who, when playing the piano, finds the best-kept secrets hidden deep in the scores. Pianist and interpreter are one. It is not only possible to recognize the piece of work he is playing, but also to recognize who is playing it. Nobody plays like him. Whoever listens to his music will say, even without seeing him: "That is Rubinstein, playing Mozart's 5$^{th}$ symphony."

Is there another level? Is there another competence level further than virtuous? Yes, and it is the one of the **Master**.

This is the last level, the peak of learning. It is, clearly, a level that only a few reach to. The master is not only sublime in regards to his actions, but also participates in the invention of the domain of action. He sets new ways to do things. He takes responsibility in mending breaks, announcing and inventing them. His performance is reflection in action and action without reflection. Everything flows harmonically.

The master does not interpret Mozart, HE IS Mozart. When he plays, music emerges and takes over everything.

This learning ladder works as a "map" that those who wish to learn should take into account so they can determine where they are standing at every time.

They should not hurry to skip any stages, as they well as not staying "comfortably put" in one level, without attempting to reach next checkpoints. Further, having the ladder present avoids making a fatal mistake: pretending higher levels than the current one.

A good apprentice has to combine urgency with patience. He will have to realize attempts, actions and exercises on time. A responsible and committed apprentice will complete the tasks without wasting time or procrastinating. But, he will also need patience to understand his own mistakes, which should be seen as the roots of a new, growing tree. When we rush in attempting to enjoy the fruits before the effort matures, if we do not give ourselves time to make mistakes, then learning will never happen, and new competences will never show.

I always remember the week that I tried skiing for the first time. It was 1981 and people in Argentina started to go crazy for skiing. I had (still do) a great friend who had been skiing since he was a child, which was a strange case back in the day. Marcelo would always tell me about his adventures on the snow, about how beautiful skiing was, while I listened, mesmerized, thinking how nice that world sounded like, but so far from my reality. I never thought of it as a possibility in my future. I would not see myself skiing.

But, motivated by my friend's enthusiasm, the numerous amount of promotions, and because it seemed really easy to go try it, I ended up signing up for a week of ski in Bariloche, Rio Negro. Full service: tickets, hotel, food, gear and classes. Everything ready to fly over to Catedral Ski Resort's white veil.

I must note I had always been a fine athlete. Each of the attempts I took at different sports had me satisfied with the results I got, at least until that moment.

Therefore, sin of youth, I faced this new challenge with the certainty that it would be easy for me. On the way to the resort, I remember looking at the runs through the bus' window. Runs I could catch a glimpse from afar, putting my attention on the highest ones, which, according to Marcelo, only the most experienced skiers could manage. In my mind, I was only a few explanations and tips away from sliding down that sleeping giant. I confess that, for a moment, I looked away from the runs and glanced at my partners, feeling pity for them, as they would never match my skills. They would have to "waste" much of their time on the easier runs, while I would be enjoying the breath taking views only seen from higher and harder ones. Then, I almost felt tender for them.

However, it turned out skiing was not so easy. As soon as I put the skies on, different sorts of difficulties came up. Naturally, I blamed the external factors, like how tight my boots were, or the fact that the snow was frozen at the base of the resort, or how inefficient and confusing my instructor's explanations were, or the illogical amount of beginners that skied by me

without letting me move. I, or more precisely, my lack of competence, had nothing to do with my failure.
Obviously, I stopped listening to my instructor. The fool did not notice I did not need his advice. I had clearly understood everything I needed to do. I already had to be skiing with the pros, had not it been for the gear, the snow, the beginners and his bad explanations. While he spoke and gave us exercises, I kept looking at the peak of the mountain, like saying "as soon as this guy is done speaking, I'm headed that way."
This all happened on a Sunday, the first of the seven days I hired for skiing. It was Wednesday morning and I had not improved a bit. I kept falling, getting bruised up, totally incapable of skiing even a few feet. Instead, my partners were ready to move on to higher, steeper, harder runs.
I said the quantity of people at the base of the resort on Sunday was so large I could barely move. On Wednesday I did not have that inconvenient anymore. I was left absolutely alone in what is commonly referred to as "fools' run".
Completely alone.
My body hurt everywhere, but it was my ego what was destroyed. I was the worst skier in my group! I was actually the worst skier amongst the approximately three thousand skiers at the mountain.
Still feeling sure I was not the one to "blame" for my failures, but the external factors, I decided one last test. I thought, "What does the instructor know? He could not see I needed a different kind of training, one fit for the gifted. His lack of vision ruined my learning."
I thought about all of this while I went up, painfully walking, the side of the "fools' run".
I walked for forty-five minutes, with the skies on my shoulders, the poles hanging on them and the boots feeling like a thousand pounds. Finally, I stopped and looked down. Despite my efforts, I did not go up that much. But, at least, I had a slope in front of me! And, I had my gear to go down! I rushed to put on my skies (of course I was actually good at this from all the times I fell, lost my skies, and had to put them again). I stuck the poles on the snow, leaned on them, and for an instant, I felt I was a skier. I even got to think "Ha, anyone looking at me now could think I have been coming down from

the top and that I stopped to enjoy the view for my last piece of run."
With my ego renewed, I picked up the poles and let Mr. Newton do his job. Pushed by him, I started gaining speed, practically none at the beginning and a little more almost immediately. "I am skiing! I knew this could not be that hard." That euphoric moment quickly passed by, when I started going faster that what I could handle and my smile turned into seriousness first and panic later. At that moment, I remembered I did not know how to turn or stop.
I had not listened to the instructor. I had not realized the exercises he suggested.
I looked, desperately, ahead. My heart stopped beating.

At the base of Catedral, where we can find the "fool's run", there is just one tree. JUST ONE. Solid, lonely and immovable. Towards it I kept sliding at an increasing speed, out of my control. The few seconds previous to the incoming catastrophe, I could only think, "if the tree does not move, we'll end up colliding." I swear that was my thought. I acknowledged the miracle of a walking tree was a little more feasible than the idea I could dodge it.
Naturally, the tree stayed put. Putting my arms ahead and turning my head around was all I could manage to do.
The collision was superb. I lost my skies, poles, sunglasses, and even my gloves! I can only imagine how funny the episode was for people skiing by, witnessing a great encounter between men and plant kingdom.
I was lucky not to be hurt. I was twenty-one and had a strong body. None of those things were merits I could take pride of.
So there I was, lying, beaten, humiliated and ashamed. But, that was the exact moment my fate was decided regards to skiing. I was on the verge of quitting. I looked at the bars on the base, where comforting, hot chocolate and an unforgettable apple pie were being served. I stared at the people sitting there, happy, warm, with dry clothes and steaming cups on their tables, and said to myself, "what am I doing here?"

I got up, got together all my gear and walked over to Tage, my favorite bar in Catedral. I looked at the mountain one last time right before my quitting decision was final.
It was then when I had an epiphany. I did not look up, where all the ones that KNEW how to ski were. I looked at the small slope I had just walked by. I saw there were a few people trying the exercises my instructor had given me earlier. I realized there was the key: If I wanted to do what people who know did (skiing on the highest runs), FIRST I HAD TO DO WHAT PEOPLE WHO DO NOT KNOW DID (exercises on the "fools' run").
I stopped looking at the experts and began to copy the beginners. With a great effort, I made some progress. I stood up, I could slide, learnt to turn and stop.
I never stopped skiing since then. I became an expert skier. I got to be one of the good ones; those who ski by, people look at to copy some movements. Now a day, there is no slope I cannot face. Every year, I go skiing with Alejandra, Kevin and Alan. And with friends. I treasure those moments so much!
I do not tell this to boast, but to make it clear that if I could learn how to ski, then anyone can learn to do anything. Anyone seeing me fiercely hugging that lonely tree would never imagine I could ever learn how to ski. Anyone who sees me today would never think I could have ever been so clumsy to crash with a tree in such a way. Learning delights.

That week meant a great deal to me. During it, I learnt to practice a sport that lets me enjoy beautiful moments with my family. But, most importantly, I learnt something decisive about learning and me. May be that is why I like skiing so much.

This story reminds me of something I wish to share with you. Just like there are different competence levels (from Beginner to Master), there also are lower levels. Many times, due to our stubbornness to not go through the effort learning requires, we end up falling on them.
Then, let us look at these Three Levels below Incompetence:

When we deny our own incompetence and our possibilities to learn, we are ready to become what I like to call "learning fools".

First, we have the "simple fool". It is someone who does not know, he knows that he does not know and denies that learning is possible. An example of a simple fool is someone who, knowing he is incompetent working a new computer, states there is no need to use it. He clings to his past competences and argues the new possibilities are pointless. The simple fool suffers this situation in silence, in loneliness.

Second, we encounter the "superfool". This is someone who brings some danger. It is someone who does not know, does not know that he does not know, and acts as if he knew. It is the classic "bull in a china shop". He moves causing disasters, but he cannot notice the consequences of his actions. Thus, the superfool does not suffer, but makes people around him suffer.

Finally, we meet the last type of this painful scale: the "criminal fool". Here, there is great danger. The criminal fool does not know, knows that he does not know and pretends to know. He is too weak and coward to state his incompetence and tends to think: "I hope nobody notices I do not know. That is the only thing I care about."

The criminal fool constantly acts in domains in which he knows he is incompetent. So, he seeks to mislead people around him. The consequences of his actions are disastrous, but he will never assume responsibility. If someone discovers him, he will undoubtedly wash his hands and blame someone else. The criminal fool spreads pain and anguish. He suffers (because he knows he does not know) and makes everyone else suffer as well (because of the consequences of his actions).

Given I do not only intend to present situations or describe characteristics, but also help in the improvement of your competence in managing the power words have, it is worth we reflect on the following questions.

The scale of competence levels as well as the three levels below incompetence let us ask some questions, whose answers will be greatly useful in practice for personal development:

Which are the domains of action that I care about, and in which of those my competence do not let me reach the goals I am looking for?
In which domains am I acting upon, even though I know I am not as competent as I should?
Can I trust and delegate in other people the actions of such domains?
Do I see suffering around me?
In which domains of action am I competent?
Is there any domain in which I might qualify as virtuous?

As we have said before, travelling the course of learning is a tough task. Each step he takes, the apprentice faces great challenges. He must beat them one by one. Failure is, at each time, a certain possibility.
However, if there is a solid commitment, if the apprentice is willing to console his ego when a battle is lost, it will be precisely that misstep what will motivate him to keep moving forward.
As Rainer Maria Rilke said: "Winning does not tempt that man. This is how he grows: by being defeated, decisively, by constantly greater things."
In his famous "Letters to a Young Poet" Rilke claims we need to hold on to what we perceive as difficult. It is our only chance for true growth. "When we win it's with small things, and the triumph itself makes us small", he said.

Following Rilke, then, we can distinguish the <u>Learning Enemies</u>:

There are many reasons why someone that has decided to seek for wisdom might pause his course. Even though he might frequently proclaim in public his need to set a learning culture, his current mental model has less to do with the one of an apprentice than the one of a know-it-all. Ignorance is still a cloak only a few are willing to wear in public.

The greatest obstacles preventing us from learning are placed within ourselves. Even those, which at first sight seem to be external, need the victim's validation to accomplish their devastating task.

Even though we have already made reference to some of the learning enemies, we are now going to present them in an organized manner, so as to "unmask" them to us.

The first of them all: **I already know**.
This enemy presents itself as arrogance. It makes its appearance every time someone rejects to admit his ignorance. It is worth to point out many times arrogance is fear's daughter. Within a culture that admires a know-it-all, it is particularly risky to accept oneself as ignorant.

A second enemy is **denying something new as new**.
In this case, the individual mixes domains up. He believes to find himself within one he already knows, when he actually is participating in a domain located in his blindness.

Then, denying something new as new is, in a way, reasonable. Human beings are constantly trying to give sense to our existence. And we give that meaning based on what we already know, in a way that lets us organize our actions within a context that seems familiar. When we "see" something new, we usually fall into confusion and perplexity. In order to move on, we pretend to "place" this new experience in a realm of comprehension we already had. But, acting this way we pay the price of not checking our assumptions. What is new is tackled as a threat to our entire coherence system. We believe we fall in contradictions. And, like Ayn Rand says: "Contradictions do not exist. Whenever you think to be facing one, check your premises."

A third enemy appears on the horizon, as a consequence of the previous one: **clinging to what is known**.
Many times, this reaction comes from lack of self-confidence. The individual repeats to himself: "I cannot learn this." He is capable of distinguishing something new as new, but sees it as something completely out of his reach. He rejects the idea of

letting what he already knows go, given that it is the only thing that gives him some sort of self-esteem.
This way, we make room for the appearance of a new enemy:

**Wanting to have everything clear, all the time.**
We have already seen confusion provokes fear. Feeling awkward due to the confusion generated by questions with no immediate answers, we claim to have all the answers at hand, always. When we wish to have everything clear, we become "addicted" to answers. An open question, without an answer, makes us feel anguished. We tell ourselves: "I do not know what is happening, and I should. It is wrong that I do not know."
We forget there is an alternative way of living questions with astonishment, telling ourselves: "I do not know what is going on, and I accept it. Of course, I would like to know, but I also like finding it out."
There is a beautiful passage in "Hello? Is Anybody There?" by Jostein Gaarder that helps us to illustrate the significance of facing questions with joy.

… I thought I had to be welcoming with him, on our planet's behalf.
- You can have an apple – I said, reaching him a green one.
It looked like it was the first time he had seen an apple. First, he smelled it, and then he dared to give it a tiny bite.
- Delicious! – He yelled, and gave it a bigger bite.
- Is it good? – I asked.
He bowed intensely.
I wanted to know that feeling of having an apple for the first time, so I asked again:
- So, how is it?
Mika bowed again. I was so confused I had to ask him:
- Why are you bowing?
Now he seemed confused. I think he doubted between bowing again or just answering me.
- Where I come from, we always bow when someone makes a fun question. – He explained. – And the deeper the question, the longer the bow.

That was the strangest thing I had ever heard. I was not capable of understanding they would bow to each other due to a question.
- So, how do you greet each other?
- We try to make up some clever question. – He answered.
- Why?
First, he bowed, and then answered:
- We try to make some clever question so that the other person bows.
I was so impressed by the answer that I bowed deeply. When I rose back up, Mika had put his thumb in his mouth again.
- Why are you bowing? – He asked, somewhat offended.
- Because you gave me quite a clever answer.
So, he told me a few words I will never forget:
- Before an answer, you are never to bow, no matter how clever and correct may it be.
I nodded. But I regret it instantly, because Mika might have believed I was bowing.
- One that bows, faces down. – Mika continued – You should never face down before an answer.
- Why not?
- An answer is always the part of the path you have already walked. Only questions can lead you forward.
Those words seemed so wise I had to pull myself backwards so that I would not bow.

Another enemy that usually appears is **the impossibility to recognize a master**. Sometimes the person notices his incompetence, but is incapable of giving authority to be taught or judged. It is as if he said: "Very well, I don't know. But, if I don't know, then who will?"

Finally, we have one last learning enemy: **impatience**.
Here, the enemy is disguised as rush. The individual trying to learn is willing to have someone teach him, but he only wants a master to answer his questions, and to do it quickly. He does not give himself or the master time for the learning process.

When facing such challenges, the internal battle the apprentice fights is truly colossal. His brightest lights and his darkest shadows engage in a battle in which only one of them will prevail. Like in the tormented Harry Haller, the unforgettable Steppenwolf presented by Herman Hesse, two "personalities" seem to clash in a never-ending battle.

On one side, there is the desire of keeping everything under control, of holding on to the security provided by what we already know. This is the voice of our "Strategic Mind", a valuable ally that whispers a tempting promise in our ears: "Listen to my advice without drifting from them and you will be safe, and live a predictable, quiet and pleasant life."
The strategic mind is, no doubt about it, a great ally. What would it be of us without it? However, it can turn into a tyrant diminishing every chance to grow.
She does not like challenges a great deal, she would rather be safe. Given she hates failure, she only embarks on small fights. We begin to assume our self-esteem of victories against lesser rivals.

But, if we pay close attention, we will also hear another voice. One that encourages us to take risks, repeating a different promise. A voice that reminds us we already are safe in our own existence.

This other contender is our own conscience, whose purpose is quite different. It invites us to meet new landscapes, facing challenges with an open ending but allow us to grow.

It is precisely that learning process where we find a magnificent scenario to solve this confrontation. Actually, the strategic mind and conscience are not rivals. It is our poor understanding of tension's nature generated between them what confuses us and shows them as irreconcilable enemies.
Conscience contains and transcends the strategic mind. Our fears shrink when we have a large conscience, in which there is room for learning's main values.

**Learning Values**

I am convinced that the transformative tools that nurture from the word's power, used without the learning values, will never achieve their purpose. It is not the lacking principle expertise what will accomplish our objectives, but the values used with those tools.

**Humbleness**

The first of these values is humbleness. Human beings design our actions based on the understanding we develop from the reality that surrounds us.

Before acting, we conceptualize situations and draw a "map" of the place we want to modify.

Of course, by necessity, this map is never identical to the real place. Its utility lies in being a simplification of a larger and more complex reality. When drawing these maps, we choose to distinguish some milestones, while we leave other aspects aside.

We do not see with our eyes, but **through** them, filtering reality with the help of our mental models.

When we observe, we put the perception filters in action. Some of these are biological, while others are determined by our mental models.

Taking all of this into account, we can say humbleness is the profound understanding that human beings have limited mental models, only interested in the reality we care about. Humbleness is to accept different people have different mental models. And, it is to understand none of those mental models can claim to perfectly represent reality.

It is worth to clarify that being humble does not mean to be fragile. One can be humble and determined. One can be assertive and, nonetheless, not at all arrogant.

Based on humbleness' value, the apprentice peacefully accepts his mental map is not perfect. Humbleness is the most effective medicine against the learning enemy hiding under the mask of arrogance.

**Compassion**
This value puts us in front of one of the greatest challenges for conscience. St. Tomas used to say that amongst all human values, compassion surely is the least understood, given that many times it is mistaken with pity.
Compassion is the deep understanding of human limits. It is the unconditional recognition that human beings do the best they can, given the mental models they posses. It is the admission that whatever fits in another human soul, has a place (at least potentially) in one self's.
It does not matter how an individual acts, he will always be answering to a logic that belongs to him, which makes his actions make sense with his objectives and with the range of possibilities that rise throughout his life.
Of course this does not mean that everything everyone else does has to be welcome. Acceptance is not pusillanimity. Before actions that represent danger, we need to defend ourselves. Compassion does not imply inaction before aggression. This is why it is so hard to live with compassion.
Acting with acceptance we can understand actions that seem strange, and explore with an open mind the explanations given by whoever takes responsibility of them. This way, we can develop a sincere and genuine curiosity used to assist those actions and explore other people's reasoning.

**Respect**
This is the paramount element for human relations. It implies to accept, unconditionally, the right to live in any chosen way. Right we have, as well as everyone else does.
Once again, I want to clarify respecting or unconditionally accepting others does not mean to validate everything they propose. Actually, it is in disagreement when respect is necessary and acting with that unconditional acceptance really makes a difference.
It is easy to respect someone else when we agree with their opinions, when they do not interfere with our objectives. But there is no merit in respecting others in such circumstance. It is when someone represents opposition when true respect becomes indispensable.

**Learning and Freedom**

We conclude this section we some thoughts on the relation between learning and freedom.
We have said learning boosts our power, that is, our capacity to generate effective actions.
And precisely, freedom feeds from those possibilities. Having more possibilities increases our options. Being free is not being bound; it is being able to choose. As long as we learn, as long as we increase our capacity to realize effective actions in different domains, we increase the quantity of available options for us. We can choose to take action because we know how to do it. Even in case of not acting upon it, our freedom has increased. Not going through with an action is a choice, not an imposition of our lack of competence.
When we do not know, we are bound to respond mechanically, with not choice at all. When we learn, we shake the burden of incompetence off, and, as there could not be other way, we face a new "burden". Learning gives us freedom, which has a cost. The cost of freedom is responsibility.

Responsibility is the ability to respond. Stripped off that dead weight produced by inability, we face the challenge of choosing how to respond, through our actions, before the given circumstances throughout our lives. Freedom and responsibility are two sides of the same coin.
When increasing our abilities, learning does not only increase our freedom, but our responsibility as well. This is the cost of living free.

## Chapter 2
### Achilles' Crossroads

In Bergen – Belsen, a region of the Lower Saxony in Germany, there was a functioning concentration camp between 1943 and 1945 that became famous overtime due to Anne Frank's death. The story we will focus on, however, deals with another prisoner, less famous, named Luigi Benigni. He was an Italian farmer and carpenter, who survived the tortures and forced works until he was freed by British troops on April 15th, 1945.

Back in Arezzo, Italy, Benigni restarted his life and in 1952 became a father, when his son, Roberto, was born. Many years later, in 1998, this child became the first actor in history to ever win an Oscar for Best Actor in a Leading Role in a foreign language. The movie, which he directed, also won Best Foreign Language Film. Only Sir Lawrence Olivier had achieved that double prince before. And nobody else did it again.

We are talking about *Life Is Beautiful*, a classic, unforgettable film that narrates the story of Guido, Nora and their son, Giosué.

The movie is inspired on the book *In the End, I Beat Hitler*, written by R.R. Salmoni and on the experiences Luigi, Roberto's father, had during his captivity at Bergen – Belsen.

This movie is indispensable for a deep understanding in the principles of the ethics of responsibility. Captured by the Nazis, Guido faces the challenge to protect his son, both physically and mentally. With death and hopelessness all around them, he makes up a game. He tells Giosué that everything that happens on that place is just a game, in which he needs to hide from the bad people. These people were, of course, the German soldiers.

Guido's lesson is one of unconditional responsibility. Knowing he cannot influence their captors' behavior, he wonders how to respond to the situation. He chooses to concentrate on saving his dearest, most loved treasure, Giosué. Guido knows he cannot choose what the German soldiers do, but he can choose what he will do as a response. Having the option to become a victim (who could have blamed him?), he chooses to become a protagonist.

The story, although might seem a contradiction (remember, contradictions do not exist. Whenever you think to be facing one, check your premises), it is full of hope. Guido's shout to live and die with unconditional freedom is invincible.

We find ourselves in front of a hero. Fragile, fearful, powerless in many of the decisions made by his captors. But, a hero that does not give up, who does not leave his values behind, who turns his problems into challenges, who does not run away from his fate but, even though he knows how tragic it is, chases it anyways.

At the end of the movie we can see Giosué on a war tank, which was "the price for winning the game". This was a tank belonging to the Allies, which saves him from the concentration camp.

Doctor Viktor Frankl had a similar story. He was a Jewish Austrian psychiatrist that was held at a concentration camp during World War II.

Doctor Frankl had and lost everything. His earnings, his job, his reputation and his family. As every other captive, even lost his name. He became just another number amongst the vast quantity of "numbers" on the death trains.

After many days on the train that was taking him to his final destination (Nazi tortures started as soon as their victims were placed in the trains, given that these did not stop until they reached one of the fatal stations. Psychic torture was the first kind of torture the captives experienced once they were taken because they did not know where they were going), he saw, precisely at the same time he got the order to step off the train, the most feared sign one could read back then: Auschwitz.

While walking to the barracks, in the midst of such horror, pain and hopelessness, Frankl made a decision. He told himself his captives could have his body, but they would never have his soul. He promised himself he would live. Live so that he would leave one day, and tell everything he had seen and bear with.

Viktor Frankl's declaration is one of the most monumental demonstrations of indomitable spirit of human beings. Freedom spirit.
I do not refer to the kind of freedom we have to choose were to be, what tasks to make or which people to share with. In such case, that would be what we can call "Conditional Freedom" because it is conditioned by results. It is the freedom we get as long as we get more of our desired results (the place, the task and the people I wish, are "things" I get, results I achieve).
No, the freedom that Doctor Frankl personifies is a more essential freedom. It is unconditional freedom, the kind that does not depend on results. It is about ALWAYS BEING ABLE TO CHOOSE. The kind of freedom that fills the spirit when one understands that, whatever happens, whatever challenge we face, human beings ALWAYS have the freedom to choose WHAT action to take, which answer to give and HOW to respond with our actions to the challenge we face.

That was Viktor Frankl's intuition when getting to the barracks. And he CHOOSES to write a book as a way of staying alive. "They can have my body, they can torture me and make me do forced labor. They can even kill me, I know that too. But, meanwhile, I choose how to live, and when choosing how to live, I choose HOW to die", he told himself.

The book he wrote under these terrible circumstances is the best piece of work I can cite as an example of proximity to the concept of Unconditional Freedom. It is titled "Man's Searching for Meaning", given that what Frankl constantly pursues during his captivity is, precisely, finding meaning to his obstinacy, giving sense to each of the actions he chooses to take. He discovers human beings need to make sense of our actions. If we cannot do it, then we do not act. Human action is not mere chance, it is not casual. It always is CAUSAL. It always has the human reasoning stamp. When we acting making no sense, we lower ourselves, we act like animals or plants. We make movements, not actions. Mere biological expressions, leaving aside the gift only human beings posses:

thinking, choosing and responding with actions filled with human sense.

Murray Rothbard, an Austrian economist, presents a similar idea on the prologue of his extraordinary book, "For a New Liberty". There, he states human beings, unlike animals and plants, cannot "simply let live". Conversely, we need to give a meaning to our actions. We do not act by instinct or chemical or biological reactions. We choose how to act. As human beings, we always choose.

It is likely that at this point you might think I am exaggerating, as well as the authors I am quoting. You might believe there are some circumstances in which you cannot choose.

Then, let me tell you about something Viktor Frankl states in his book.

Doctor Frankl gives a tale about his days as captive at Auschwitz. He tells us about the feeling of own life precariousness that every prisoner constantly felt. There were no explanations for how poorly they were treated; it just happened. They meant the end for word use. The captives woke up every morning not knowing whether they would survive until the end of the day. Some could not stand that situation and, both mentally and physically exhausted, they just let themselves die. Frankl says it was not hard to tell what prisoners had given up: on the beginning of each day, Nazis would distribute the daily portions of bread to each of the captives. The prisoners that were willing to live at least one more day would safe half portion to eat it after forced labor, at the end of the day. Whoever was ready to die would eat all of it in the morning. That way, they sentenced the lack of future. With no future ahead giving meaning to their actions, they chose to die.

It is hard to think of a more unjust and cruel situation than this one. And, nonetheless, in the midst of that terror, Viktor Frankl discovers unconditional freedom. Even in that circumstance, he could choose between eating the entire portion of bread or saving some for later.

He realized he could choose to live. And when someone chooses to live, even if he dies later on, he will have lived intensely each moment throughout his lifetime.

Then, we begin to see a great connection: the one between freedom and responsibility. It actually is about two sides of the same coin. There is no responsibility, which is the ability to respond, without the freedom to choose a response. And there is no freedom if we do not take responsibility for the consequences of our choices.

Lets go back, then, to the previous thought about whether saying human beings can always choose is correct. There is a focal point when talking about responsibility and freedom.
Lets travel back in history, to the Victorian times. More precisely, lets go back to the beginning of the decade during the 1890's. Imagine being in Bistriz, Eastern Europe. Jonathan Harker is telling us a strange story. Yes, we are talking about a classic in literature: "Dracula". Since it was published in 1898, and a year later in USA, Bram Stoker's eternal novel has not stopped circulating and being read by people around the globe. Besides being one of the first Gothic novels, where mystery, terror, and love take place, the book tells us about customs, inventions, social relations and the role of women in England towards the end of the XIX century.
The moment in the novel we will use to illustrate the certain possibility of choosing human beings have, is told in the first chapter.
Jonathan Harker, a young, real estate agent from London, is about to travel in a carriage. His final destination is Count Dracula's Castle, placed in the easternmost region of Transylvania, close to Bukovina.
It is May fourth, Saint George's day. In Eastern Europe, this is the equivalent to Halloween.
The carriage Harker gets in after leaving the Golden Crown Hotel in Bistriz is taking him to the Borgo Pass. There, another carriage is waiting for him, one owned by the Count, which will take him to the Castle.
Nothing major happened during the first part of the trip. When they get to the Pass, Harker steps off and stays alone, looking how the carriage that had brought him there now rides away at a fast pace. Seconds later, as if it came from nowhere, Count Dracula's carriage appears. He sees a spooky driver, with an

inhuman strength (Harker tells in his diary the man took his three bags with one hand and put them on the carriage making no effort at all). The night is rainy and cold, the path dark and, the deeper they get into the Carpathians, it gets dangerously narrower. Along with this scene, wild wolves escorted the carriage throughout the entire ride.

After long hours sitting on the carriage, close to midnight, the carriage stops and the strange driver (later on we find out it is Dracula himself) tells Harker to get off. All there is in front of him is a narrow path that leads to the Castle's door.

Soaked, frightened, extremely cold, the young man knocks on the door. After waiting for some minutes, during which Jonathan is practically sure he is going to get eaten by the wolves, the door opens and he sees the Count. The words Dracula uses to welcome Harker have become inmortal, and they conceive an invaluable message about the capacity to choose and the impossibility to escape the consequences of our actions.

-"Welcome to my humble abode, Mr. Harker." – says the Count – "Enter on your free will, and leave some of the happiness you bring, outside."

That is the "greeting" that the host gives to his guest. Notice that the vampire does NOT make Harker come into the castle. He offers the chance to enter, but Harker can reject it. Of course, rejecting it has its consequences. He could be devoured by the wolves, for example. Leaving some of the happiness is the price of entering the castle, as the Count manifests.

If you choose to stay outside, I will do nothing to stop you. But if you decide to come in, it will be my castle, my rules.

And there is Jonathan Harker, having to choose between one or the other. But, always choosing. And paying the price for his own choices.

Many times we face this kind of dilemmas during our life. And we believe we are not capable of choosing. We feel we are "obliged" to take a path.

But, remembering Viktor Frankl in real life, and Guido and Harker in fiction, we can understand we can ALWAYS choose.

Some times between options that are equally undesirable. Then, we will have to try paying the lower price.
But, we will always have the chance to choose. Free.
And we will always face the need to take care of the consequences of our choices. Responsible.

May be, this is why Jean Paul Sartre used to say human beings are condemned to be free.

It is not by putting the "blame" on others, or external factor, how we should respond to the challenges we face. It is by being responsible in order to take actions that lead us to better circumstances.
The Ethics of Responsibility suggests an unavoidable question: **How am I supposed to respond, through my actions, to the challenges I face in life?**
The answer for this question conceives the effectiveness and happiness we can reach. Of course, both goals are crucial. Even in the midst of our difficulties, we need to find answers. There is no use in complaining about something we did not deserve, or something that could have been. We will not be able to modify what we do not like acting this way. Only by understanding that in every crisis there is an opportunity to change and learning, and acting upon it, is how we can shape our world in a way that looks bit more similar to what we desire.

**The power of explanations**

Every time we observe what happens, human beings create an explanation. We are never "passive" viewer of what is happening. Instead, our watch always focuses on the details we care about, and we make an analysis based on our experiences and stories.
Of course, and precisely because of that, our explanations do not talk about THE truth. They are a narrative articulation, a story that rises as an answer to the questions we ask ourselves as viewers of what is happening.
Nonetheless, we ought to be careful. The fact an explanation does not represent "THE" truth does not mean it lacks

importance. Quite contrarily, these explanations are decisive when it comes to reaching, or not, our objectives, and when reaching for efficiency and harmony.
It is important to understand we are used to considering just one validation criterion for our explanations: Truth criterion. But, there is another one: Utility criterion.
Explanations are not "objective" truths, but articulations referring, or not, to an action. Then, it is possible to adopt other lights to show the way for our decisions. While our explanations are not "true", or better yet, that we cannot "measure" our explanations with a truth criterion, it does not mean we cannot prefer to choose some and discard others.

When we discard the "truth" criterion and consider, instead, the "utility" criterion, we can choose those explanations that result more useful to us, without taking into account if they reflect THE truth or not.

A "good" explanation is one that provides utility, which serves our purposes.
The characteristics of a good explanation are the following:
1. They serve the purposes of the person explaining it.
2. They are congruent with other explanations expressed by the same person.
3. They are coherent with the values previously declared by that individual.

Therefore, for a unique situation there might be a set of different explanations.
In order to choose one and discard others, we need to make sure that the one we choose is composed by those three characteristics.
It may even happen that more that one explanation for a given situation is composed by these characteristics. On this case, we will analyze which one serves our purposes the best. We will chose the one that opens more possibilities for action and the one we will give the greatest success percentage towards reaching our goals.

There is no doubt everyone creates their explanations according to their personal interests. And this is absolutely legitimate.

It is possible that these concepts seem "too eclectic", or that it opens the possibility to accept any explanation given in a certain situation.

But, we should dissipate this doubt when realizing we have demanded a "goodness" condition for our explanations.

We have said an explanation is "good" if it COMPLIES WITH THE THREE CHARACTERISTICS PRESENTED.

If this happens, there should not be a problem with:
a. Someone having multiple explanations for a determined situation.
b. Different people having different explanations for a given situation.

This is natural and, in fact, happens daily.

Each explanation is like a map. I would say we all agree in saying there is no sense in arguing whether a demographic map is "better" than a geological one. It all depends on WHAT is it going to be used for.

The same happens with explanations. The key aspect lies on the congruence of our three "golden" rules for explanations.

Besides the specific goals for each situation, when expressing an explanation, the individual seeks one of the broader objectives:
1. Avoiding the question, without committing to the problem
2. Declaring the problem involved is a challenge and being prepared to intervene.

We will call the first kind of explanations "soothing explanations". The second kind are called "mobilizing explanations".

Whoever gives a soothing explanation seeks to ease the frustration and anguish provoked by not being able to get a certain result.

Whoever generates a mobilizing explanation, instead, seeks to respond to a challenge according to his values and interests, trying to modify the raised situation and accomplish the goal.
When we choose soothing explanations, we take the victim's role.
When we choose mobilizing explanations, we take the protagonist's role.

Once again, the cinema helps us to illustrate the idea.
*The Shawshank Redemption* is a film released in 1994, directed by Frank Darabont, starring Tim Robbins and Morgan Freeman. It tells Andy Dufresne's story, an accountant accused of his wife and her lover's murder.
The same way we talked about *Life is Beautiful*, we find ourselves in an unfair confinement situation (something we discover halfway through the film).
And, once again, this is the story of someone who chooses to be the protagonist instead of becoming a victim. He chooses to create a mobilizing explanation and to generate actions that allow him to improve his condition throughout his captivity and give him hope to escape.
In many of its scenes, *The Shawshank Redemption* shows how the creation of powerful stories, of mobilizing explanations, can make a person feel moments of absolute freedom, despite being confined inside the walls of a maximum-security prison.
Out of all these scenes, the one that happens on the roof of one of the prison's pavilions, while Dufresne observes his mates drink a few cold beers (award for fixing the roofs) under the hot sun of a summer midday, encloses the most wonderful key of human existence: the certainty of the unbeatable human spirit.

There is no doubt that a soothing explanation allows whoever uses it to show his anguish and frustration for not being able to reach his goals, blaming others or the "circumstance".
Trying to be seen as not "guilty", the individual desperately generates explanations that exonerate him from blame for the results, as well as all responsibility for what needs to be done to respond to such results.

When looking for that peace of mind "innocence" gives, he pays the price of immobility. The victim is not "guilty" but does not have the power to get out of that situation either. Soothing explanations, as well as medicines that seek for the same outcome, calm emotions in a short term, but do not allow thinking clearly about the nature of the actions that might get us out of an unfavorable situation. When we consume soothers (either pills or explanations), we momentarily calm our anguish, but we lose levels of consciousness about the problem we are really involved in, puzzling our understanding of the situation, making it harder to overcome it.

Soothing explanations usually rise from the creation the individual makes when attempting to answer a set of questions he asks himself. Such questions are:
What happened to **ME**?
Who affected **ME** so negatively?
What have they done to **ME**?
Who did this to **ME**?
What did **I DESERVE** they did?
Who has the **BLAME** for what happened?
What should the people that affected **ME** do in order to fix the damage they have done to **ME**?
How should others act in order to compensate the injustice of their actions towards **ME**?

Of course **OTHERS** can be either one person, or a group of people or own "impersonal" reality ("circumstances").
A victim does not care about that. All he cares about is to make clear that the situation he is in does not correspond to his actions or merits.

Soothing explanations are seen everywhere. Expressions like "my husband is so difficult, he never cares about what I care', or "my students are so lazy, they never care to study what I ask them to", or "our clients are incomprehensible, they never appreciate the quality of the services we offer, nor they value our efforts", are examples of this kind of explanations.

It is very important to clarify such examples can be perfectly congruent (that is, totally well-founded), but present a fatal inconvenient: **THEY DO NOT GENERATE ACTIONS THAT ALLOW US TO MODIFY THE SITUATION.**

The source of power to change what does not satisfies us lies in taking responsibility. Whoever sees oneself as protagonist, someone that **HAS THE CAPACITY TO RESPOND**, suffers the cost of feeling the pain for being the one who does not get what he is looking for (not others), but also has the determination to get out of that situation.

This path is definitely harder, but more promising as well. It is about incorporating the Ethics of the Protagonist. This way, the person leaves the soothing explanations and the negative judgments about others behind, and focuses on the search of possibilities for action aiming towards desired goals.

The protagonist realizes he cannot choose what happens to him, but he can ALWAYS choose how to respond (through his actions) to what happens to him.

Even when one is not the "cause" of a negative situation, one can always make room to respond in order to attend own interests and objectives.

Just like Andy Dufresne does it.

Mobilizing explanations rise as the expression of answers we find to the following questions:
What challenges am I facing?
What are the **FACTS** about what happened?
What did **I** do in such circumstances?
What objectives did **I** pursue when doing what I **DID**?
Which of **MY** interests, objectives or desires are affected by this challenge?
Which new actions can I **TAKE** to get out of this situation?
Can those actions put me close to **MY** primary objectives?
Should I change such objectives?
Are these new actions aligned with **MY** main values?
Besides the actions I can take to get out of this situation, are there others I can take to minimize the damage?
Who can I help me out?

How do I base **MY** opinions of trust on those I have chosen to help me out?
What did I learn from this experience?

This set of questions, **PLUS** the answers we give, put us in the spot of the protagonist of the situation.
Our fate is now in our hands, not in others' or "circumstances".
Even though there is no action that can guarantee absolute success given every result always depends on contingency, paying the price of being responsible gives us the privilege of our own freedom.
It is a freedom that will not be the conditional freedom of always getting what we want (we call it conditional because it depends on the achievement of results, always exposed to the conditions imposed by contingency), but the unconditional freedom of always being able to choose the answers we give before each challenge we face.

On People's Square of Pekin, Calaf observes the previous moments to the execution of the young Prince of Persia. The Prince is about to pay with his life the attempt to win the heart of the Emperor of China's daughter. Anyone who wishes to marry the Princess must pass one test: answer three questions correctly. In case of failing, the price to pay is death.
The Prince of Persia has failed and is about to be executed. The crowd gathered on the Square is moved by seeing the quiet, handsome, young man and asks for mercy. Calaf, also a Prince, disguised amongst the people, adds to this claim, rejecting such a cruel act.
Then, the Princess gets out of her chamber and, with a merciless gesture, orders the executioner to carry on with his duty. The Princess walks into her chamber immediately after this.
That moment was enough for Calaf to fall helplessly in love with her. From then on, he is to face his destiny.

This is the first act in "Turandot", Giacomo Puccini's posthumous Opera. The rest of the three-act play tells the way in which Calaf ignores the desperate claims of his father, the

King of the Tartars, to forget the idea of passing the test of the three questions. No one has ever answered those three questions correctly. Everyone that dared to love Turandot has died.

But, it turns out Calaf is determined, but also intelligent. And, one by one, he answers all questions correctly. Then, the unthinkable happens: Turandot denies complying with her part of the deal, rejecting Calaf.

In light of this unexpected scenario, Calaf proposes a new deal. It is him who now proposes a puzzle. Given he was incognito in Pekin, nobody knows him or his name. If Turandot finds it out before sunrise, then she will be pardoned for breaking the previous deal and Calaf will be executed.

Turandot quickly accepts the proposal. At sunset, the Princess orders all of her soldiers to explore and find out his name. There will be a death penalty for anyone who knows his name and does not say it. This is the climax on the opera. Calaf sings one of the most famous and beautiful arias in the history of music: *Nessun Dorma*.

Calaf sings: "None shall sleep! /Even you, oh Princess, /in your cold room, /watch the stars, /that tremble with love/ and with hope. /But my secret is hidden within me, /[…] On your mouth I will tell it, /When the light shines. /And my kiss will dissolve the silence that makes you mine!"

On the first lights of the new day, Calaf uncovers who he is: "I am Calaf, son of Timur", he tells her while kissing her. Calaf has decided to pay with his life the price of his love kiss.

This story, like every other story that is worth telling, talks about a beautiful woman. But it also talks about victims and protagonists.

Calaf, who put his life in stake when submitting to the test of the three questions, far from playing the victim's role when Turandot betrays him by breaking the deal, takes the role of the protagonist and designs a new challenge. He knows he cannot choose what the Princess will do. But, he also knows he can choose what to do before the situation he is in. And he chooses to find love, to warm Turandot's cold heart. He raises the bet and accepts the consequences of his choice.

He does not generate a soothing explanation like: "She betrayed me, and I did not deserve that. If she does not change her decision, there is nothing I can do."
Instead, he asks himself: "what can I do now to make her change her opinion and prove her word?" When answering this question, he comes up with a mobilizing explanation.
It is worth watching and listening to this opera, to know the end of the story and Calaf and Turandot's fate.

These kinds of explanations give power, since they give the chance to generate effective actions. Of course, they carry with them a price to pay: making a COMMITMENT with OWN ACTIONS, and ACCEPTING the RESPONSIBILITY for the RESULTS of such actions. The PROTAGONIST is unconditionally committed to implementing all the actions oriented to accomplishing his objectives, and is takes responsibility for the consequences (results) of such actions.
Acting this way, he is not guaranteed achieving the results. That is the truth. NOTHING guarantees results in our lives. We are contingent beings. But, this way of living DOES secure DIGNITY, which is nothing else than doing everything at hand to get my results, in coherence with my values.

When articulating goals and values, people come up with a strategy. When we do not get what we want, we stop blaming others or circumstances, and prepare to act.
The protagonist takes control of his fate. And fulfills it.
Primo Levi beautifully illustrates it on his Gedal Song:
"If I don't take care of myself, then, who will? If this isn't the way, then, what is? If not now, then, when?"
Some explanations, as we have seen, put us in the place of the victim. Other, make us the protagonist.
But, sometimes, life puts us in a bigger problem. The decision deals with the highest values. And it is then when the hero's spirit rises.
When Achilles, King of Myrmidons, was invited by Agamemnon and Menelaus to be part of the expedition to Troy, with the clear objective of getting Helena back, he was filled with doubts. Achilles was a warrior, the biggest, best one of this time. Unbeaten and invulnerable. Brave and daring.

There was a fire within him for battling. However, he did not like Agamemnon and did not care too much whether Menelaus got Helena back. He was not sure to join the Greek army.
Then, Achilles had a talk with his mother, the Goddess Thetis. During their conversation, she tells him an oracle has warned her about her son's fate:
-" *If you decide not to participate in the war against Troy, you'll live many years, you'll get married, you'll have beautiful children and you'll rule as a wise King, loved by every Myrmidon. You'll have a long life and, when you die, your children will remember you, as well as their children. But, then, when they have died, your story will slowly fade away. If, on the other hand, you choose to join the invasion in Troy, you'll have all the glory, a thousand years will go be and the entire world will remember who Achilles was, the greatest warrior, the King of the Myrmidons. But, there is a big cost for this glory. You will die in Troy."*

Achilles, then, makes up his mind: he goes to Troy. He realizes a hero is not just the protagonist of his own life. A hero, through his actions, is inspiring and protagonist of other people's lives. He honors his values, even when there is a big cost. Achilles proves a hero does not avoid his fate: he fulfills it.

A final thought about actions, goals and results from the Ethics of the Protagonist's point of view.
The choices we constantly make, DO NOT DETERMINE the results we get. They barely INFLUENCE them. On the difference there is between determining and influencing, lies the contingent nature of our lives.
But, the fact that our actions do not determine our results, does not mean we ought to forgo they DO influence them. And that influence could be decisive in our lives. It is better not to forget, in order not to use contingency as an excuse for inaction. There is much to do. And once we have acted, we have to accept the results. And live in peace with contingency. Battles will be lost, but not the war itself. And, by need, those will not be plenty.

Being protagonists of our own lives, we will keep our calm when luck strikes. We will do everything at hand, and we will accept what we cannot control. And we will look our future with optimism.
As the Sufi proverb says:

*Trust your God.*
*And tightly tie your horse.*

# Chapter 3
## Living Poets Society
*In loving memory of Robin Williams*

*"We don't read and write poetry because it's cute. We read and write poetry because we are members of the human race. And the human race is filled with passion...medicine, law, business, engineering, these are noble pursuits and necessary to sustain life. But poetry, beauty, romance, love, these are what we stay alive for."*

*Dead Poets Society* is an American film from 1989, directed by Peter Weir, starring Robin Williams, with his unforgettable role as Literature Professor John Keating. The movie's main topic revolves around the greatest ability a human being can develop: seizing life.

The professor uses literature as a way to show his students the necessity of living each moment with an intensity as a result of a very special kind of urgency. The urgency of knowing we are finite beings, and realizing each moment is unique and fleeting. And they deserve being seized.

The entire movie is, actually, a great tribute to a generation of poets and poetesses that rose in America during the first half of the XIX Century: a group of passionate young people that founded a new Athens, honoring freedom and the beauty of being alive. Lead by Walt Whitman (cited plenty of times during the film) and Ralph Waldo Emerson (author of the Intellectual Declaration of Independence), these poets and poetesses achieved giving passion a place within intellect. They highlighted the beauty, harmony, enjoyment wishes and constant search for happiness as crucial elements of our existence. They discovered the right to live fully and in freedom. And, what is decisive for the purposes of this chapter, they built a bridge between intellect and passion. For first time in modern history, a group of intellectuals sung to physical enjoyment. They proved poetry (clear product of human reason and mind) could sing to the body and emotions. And, this way, they opened the first gap in an iron mental model, which irreconcilably divides reason from emotion.

During a long time, before and after the rise of this generation, the most famous mental model had been backed on Blas Pascal's claim: "The heart has reasons that reason cannot understand." Looking for, perhaps, an incisive difference from the rest of the living species, humans enthroned reason, in detriment of emotional control.

I would like to say I completely agree with reason being the differentiating element for men and women. Existing as rational beings is not only a unique characteristic, but also an obligation for human beings. Renouncing reason is renouncing to our own humanity. Thinking and reflecting are abilities, as well as responsibilities, of human existence.

But, the fact that it is our duty to use rationality is not opposite to being emotional beings too. The fatal error, the lie that blurs our understanding of human phenomenon, is believing rationality and emotion are opposed.

Actually, the heart has reasons that reason can know. And, not only knows, it also provokes.

This chapter intends to build a bridge between both dominions. We will "deactivate" that alleged dichotomy between reason and passion. We will try to prove the division between mind (rational) and emotion, is ant natural and has very little to do with the true nature of human phenomenon.

**Scholar Intelligence and Emotional Intelligence**

After considerable developments achieved in the area of cognitive science, added to the ones in neuroscience and psychology, it has been proved there are multiple types of intelligence.

One of the most elaborate works can be found on Harvard's psychologist and researcher Professor Howard Gardner's "Theory of Multiple Intelligence".

Besides his excellent findings in the area, what we really care about on this chapter is the definition Professor Gardner elaborates for intelligence.

"Intelligence", Gardner says, "is the capacity to solve problems."

At first sight, it seems to be an extremely simple definition, without much value. Nonetheless, it proposes a link between "problems" and certain "capacity".
There is another reason why this definition is valuable.
First, it is quite broad. It suggests all capacity to solve problems must be acknowledged as intelligence.
Second, it is quite practical. When linking intelligence with CAPACITY to solve, leaving aside intellectual speculations, it places the idea of intelligence in a practical domain. If you solve a problem, it is due to intelligence.

Perhaps, the reader might notice the definition of "intelligence" Gardner gives is absolutely aligned with the one we have presented in the beginning of this book. In both, intelligence is related with the capacity of reaching objectives.

Of course, we will not stop at this definition; we will try to add some ideas and clarify other matters.
It is worth anticipating we are going to call intelligence a capacity of realizing own actions. If a problem gets solved by external actions, we shall not say we have been "intelligent" to solve. Intelligence also suggests an intention, desire and wish for changing, and of course, the capacity to make it happen.
Therefore, it is not because of intelligence every time a problem gets solved.
As we said earlier, there are three different types of intelligence. For example, there is the logical-mathematical intelligence, which lets us understand the nature of an arithmetic problem, solve a strategy dilemma or comprehend a measure pattern.
Diversely, linguistic intelligence is used for reading comprehension, or completing a crossword.
Then, emotional intelligence will be the one that helps us **DISTINGUISH THE CAUSES OF A CERTAIN EMOTION, DIFFERENTIATE SAID EMOTION, AND GENERATE ACTIONS THAT LET US CONTROL IT ACCORDING TO OUR OBJECTIVES.**

If we stick to Gardner's definition, it is clear learning to identify the causes of an emotion, being capable of differentiating it from others, and having the ability to act on it to change it in order to serve our purposes, is a "capacity to solve a problem." On this case, an emotional "problem".

Once again, I believe it is worth to highlight this way of understanding what "emotional intelligence" is, is coherent with the definition of "intelligence" we have stated. The "distinctions" we refer to, that is, the capacity to distinguish, is referred to the different causes of a particular emotion, and using this capacity of distinguishing to obtain the results we have set, is linked in the case of emotional intelligence with the goal of managing such emotion.

It is very important to understand that, in the case of managing emotions, staying true to the values we have chosen to guide our ethic is highly important, given this will mark the difference between "managing" and "manipulating" emotions. One who is "manipulative" does not care for values or lives by honorable ethics.

Here, I would like to make a side note about "problems". What we call "problems" is nothing else than mere narrative articulations about what we see is happening. When talking about the power of explanations, we referred to this matter.

What really happens when a problem "comes up", is that some event we cannot control (it is out of our reach, it is "external") disrupts our path to our objectives.

Before this kind of situations, we usually generate an explanation of what is happening, a narrative articulation about the facts that make us understand what happens.

The first concept we need to highlight is that "problems" do not come up by themselves, but are created due to our own explanations of certain situations.

When an unexpected event arises, disrupting the way to our goals, and we add an explanation composed by negative opinions about what happened, we face a problem.

It is crucial to realize problems are not out there; they do not come from external factors. What does exist out there, and is an external reality, is a FACT. When we articulate a fact in a certain way, we turn them into problems.

It is also important to understand that saying "actual" problems do not exist (rather, they are our own "inventions") it is not the same as claiming "actually", "problems" do not exist.
Of course they exist. They exist once we create them. They exist with the same strength ideas come from. And, in the human realm, ideas exist and are extremely powerful. It is not reasonable to deny interpretations (ideas) exist and have consequences in the material world.

**Once again, a digression: Santa Claus' cruel deceit**

Lets drift away for a moment from the focus on emotional intelligence, to dig deep in the "existence" of ideas.
On his book "Zen and the Art of Motorcycle Maintenance", Robert Pirsig posts all human beings believe in ghosts.
What are a ghost's characteristics? – Pirsig questions.
Well then, ghosts are "something" we cannot see, nor touch, nor smell. They do not have a color, or weight, or volume. It seems as if they fully fill the "form" of something that does NOT exist.
However, the ghosts in fantastic literature "do things" in the material world. They disrupt it, they disturb it. It is precisely this disruption of reality, this disturb of the material world what make allegations for their existence.
Ideas, those omnipresent concepts all human beings believe in, also lack color, volume and weight. They cannot be touched, or be seen, or be smelled. Nonetheless, it is clear they have consequences over the material world. They disrupt it, they disturb it, they change it.
Therefore, ideas "ghosts" we all believe in. We do not only believe in them, but create them, and then let them show us the world and guide us.
As Robert Frost says:
"The eye itself does not have the capacity to see.
We do not see a thing until we get the IDEA.
Until the idea is planted in our mind…
And then, we cannot see anything but it."

A quite clear example of the existence and power of ideas, is the one that let us look into one of the deepest mysteries of our childhood.
Does Santa Claus really exist?
The answer is not insignificant, since if negative, it pushes parents to face a moral dilemma: should I lie to my son and assure Santa exists? Or, is it better to sacrifice a few years of hope, in sake of not telling them a lie?

From my point of view, there is but one Christmas lie.
I was about nine or ten when I was told Santa Claus did not exist.
I remember thinking: "If Santa does not exist, then that means the Tooth Fairy does not exist either." How blatantly had I been lied to!
I remember feeling a wave of disappointment and sorrow crushing me. A strike that hit my innocence, burying me six feet under.
I also remember running to my room, checking toys, books and other gifts that had been placed under our Christmas trees throughout my short span of life.
Those gifts, whose existence was undeniable, were evidence contradicting such terrible news. There they were, arguing in favor of the existence of the bulky, jolly, old man in a red suit.

I state in such moment I faced the greatest, most cruel lie regarding Christmas:
The lie in saying Santa Claus does not exist.
This was, actually, the most ignoble lie of all.
Because, ladies and gentleman, lets say it out loud, once and for all: Santa Claus EXISTS.
Of course, we are not talking about "someone made in flesh and bone." Santa Claus is an idea.
And ideas exist.
Ideas are a crucial portion of our lives, and they are what we mostly care about. Tomorrow, the future, happiness, for example, are ideas, concepts. Creations of our own mind. Have you ever seen "tomorrow"? Of course you have not. Because tomorrow is something that only exists in our mind.

It is an idea. When "tomorrow" finally arrives, it becomes "today".
But it is precisely the idea "there is tomorrow" what moves us, what demands from us, what excites us.
The same happens when it comes to Santa Claus. Nobody has ever seen him. Simply because he is an idea, another creation of our mind.
And, same as every other powerful idea, he moves and excites us.
Millions of people around the world come and go during the end of each year, driven by the idea of Santa Claus. They give and get presents; they show and receive love.
Can one be so cynical, skeptical and miserable to reject this undeniable reality?
Ideas cannot be perceived. But, it is possible to show and appreciate the consequences of their existence.
Throughout history of mankind, powerful ideas have made the path for men and women.
And the world we live in, with its flaws, but with its hopeful energy of beauty and kindness too, is the result of thousands, millions of ideas.
I believe it is necessary to leave cynicism behind, and tell the world the truth about Santa Claus.
Let everyone know Santa Claus exists.
He lives within the unyielding search for the promised gift, within the magic of imagining a bright light in the skies is the sled landing on the roofs nearby, within the love overflowing in each Christmas carol told.
Lets fight against the small army of the misbelievers. Lets prevent the "guardians of the tangible truth" from getting away with it. Lets not be fooled into believing Santa does not exist.
Or, even worse, may them mercilessly and cruelly kill him. Lets not let them, "the legend wreckers" as my friend Alejandro Dolina would say, win.
Santa Claus exists.
To me, he has always existed, and always will do, in the memory of my father, my mother and my grandparents, stealthily carrying and hiding those unforgettable gifts that

magically appeared before me, under the tree, confirming the miracle of eternal love.

**Going back to "emotional problems"**

Then, we find ourselves at a point in which we have realized emotional problems exist. These happen when we feel an emotion that leads us to taking certain actions, and we are not capable of coping with the emotion or the actions we take as an answer to it.
Emotional intelligence, then, is the capacity we develop to act on these problems successfully.

The emotional domain in which we act is composed by two types of emotions: own and external. Undoubtedly, they both influence our results.
Emotional intelligence lets us intervene on both kinds successfully. Ergo, someone who is emotional intelligent will be able to control not only personal emotions, but other people's as well.
Then, we face what seems a moral dilemma. It is easy to acknowledge it is totally legitimate to try controlling own emotions. However, when it comes to controlling other people's emotions, we quickly believe this means to "manipulate" others. And, this thought carries a moral dilemma: is it legitimate to do this?
The dilemma dissolves when we remember our definition of "INTELLIGENCE" presented in the Introducción of this book, the one that invokes ethic and values and we understand manipulating emotions (which is always dishonest) is completely different from controlling.
The great difference is "manipulating" implies trying to generate an emotion in someone else to serve our own purposes, while not being willing to experience such emotions ourselves.
Whoever manipulates, proposes an emotional state in which he suspects other people's emotions are useful for own purposes, without sharing the emotion, without experiencing it and without respecting other people's motives. Whoever manipulates, cheats. He pretends to have an emotion. He lies

with his speech. He contradicts one of the basic precepts of healthy human relations, and one of the most appreciated and necessary values: Sincerity.

Whoever controls an emotion, instead, proposes an emotional space, he tries to make his listener experience an emotion that is useful for his purposes, but is **ABSOLUTELY WILLING** to experience it himself as well, to experience it the same way he expects the other person to.

He does not lie, cheat or pretend. He has an honest speech, looks for his own benefit and respects his listener's values and objectives. And he unconditionally respects the other person's choice about accepting or not the proposed emotionality. Clearly, this is an absolutely legitimate way of operating. Every human being has the inalienable right to pursue his own benefit, while respecting that right for everyone else during the process.

**Emotion dynamics**

There is a deep relation between the emotions we experience and the actions we are capable of taking.

The origin of the term "emotion" refers to this relation, as explained in Corominas' Etymological Dictionary. In it, we discover the word EMOTION is quite a "new" term in our language. It appears in 1604, but it becomes more constantly used much later, during the XIX century. It comes from the French word "emotion", coming from "emouvoir", which means to move or be moved. The relation between emotion and action begins to come about. "Mouvoir" (move) and "emotion" are very similar.

Within a totally different area, like Biology and Neuroscience, Humberto Maturana confirms this relation every time he claims "emotions are predisposition for action".

Then, the following question rises: How does one verify this relation? A question that derives to others, such as: Is it possible to determine the origin of an emotion? And, can we modify the emotions we experience? Or better yet, do we have the chance to "design" emotions? Lets see if we can find answers for these questions.

In order to do that, lets use a text written by Michael Graves, in which he imagines someone who goes for a walk on the mountain on a certain day. As he walks, he observes the nature; he stops to look at the trees, to listen the birds sing. Far away, he can listen to the river running against the rocks. A few minutes into the walk, while his trail almost vanishes behind him, he begins to think about a possible project, likely to be initiated in the next few days. He feels happy, optimistic; the project thrills him, he believes once it is finished, it will open doors that at the time had remained closed. He smiles.

At that instant, he sees a snake slithering to him, on the middle of the trail, a few meters from him. Suddenly, this observation takes him to a completely different experience. He is scared, his heart begins to pump quicker; he asks himself if he will have enough room to dodge the snake or if he will have to turn around. His possibilities now have taken an unexpected twist. Fear has taken over him. There are no rivers anymore, or birds or plans. There only is a snake and a path that suddenly became to narrow.

Analyzing this short story, we can draw a first conclusion about emotion dynamics: there always exists a fact that creates them.

Even though when it seems obvious, it is essential for understanding the emotional world that we clearly state this intuition. **EVERY EMOTION IS ORIGINATED FROM SOME FACT.** That means, emotions are not "something that happen" without any explanation or clear origin, as we have been told many times. They do not originate from mysterious, inscrutable reasons, nor they come "impregnated" with our character or "personality". They do not happen "just because". They always have a reason, an origin. A fact that unchains them.

This fact can be provoked by an external force, or it can be the result of own actions taken previously. In any case, it is about something we get to, and that we need to take care of.

On Graves' story, the emotions of peace and aspiration the person experiences at the beginning are a clear example of what we are saying. An external fact (or as in this case, a set of facts), like trees, birds' singing or the river, provokes the person to feel calm. It is clear this person cannot control whether there are trees or not, whether the birds sing, or the river clashing against the rocks. All he can do is to articulate those external facts and, based on that articulation, which DOES belong to him, he experiences the emotion we call serenity or peace.

Meanwhile, another fact, which is internal, unchains the emotion of aspiration. Such fact is his own thought, that conversation he quietly has with himself.

His future plans provoke him to feel ambitious or aspiring. If there were no such plans, or if the person did not remember them at that time, the emotion would not happen.

It is also logical to think, and in fact this is what happens, that experiencing the emotion of serenity predisposes him for reflection, and reflecting about his plans provokes him the emotion of aspiration.

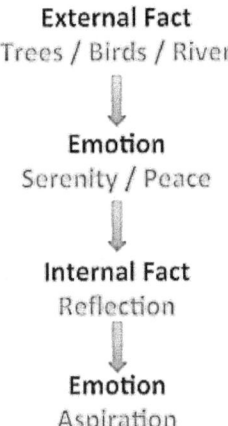

The figure above is absolutely congruent with Maturana's statement: emotions are predisposition for action. On this case, the <u>emotion</u> of **serenity** predisposes the <u>action</u> of **reflecting**. And, it is also coherent with the first principle of emotion dynamics: emotions are unchained by perceiving facts. In our case, the <u>perception</u> of trees, birds' songs and the sound coming from the river.

Sticking to our example, suddenly we see a new external fact, the snake, unchains totally different emotions.
Our character cannot choose whether the snake appears or not. It is an external fact out of his control.
And, given the articulation he makes of this new external fact (the snake is dangerous), his perception unchains the emotion of fear.

Before continuing with emotion dynamics, it is worth to point out some of the aspects we are discussing.
Firstly, we must realize the articulation of our character makes about the appearance of a snake on his way **IT IS NOT THE ONLY POSSIBLE ONE**. The same way he tells himself "the snake is dangerous", someone that is more used to walking around the mountain, thus, more familiarized with the presence of snakes, could say: Oh! A snake. I am going to try not to step on it, I don't want to hurt the poor animal." On this case, the person sees no danger before the presence of the snake, and his only emotion is that of worrying about not hurting the harmless reptile. There could even be someone that delights on the opportunity of seeing a snake. On this case, such person would think" "Oh, good luck! A snake! I'll try to catch it so I can eat it tonight." His articulation about the snake's appearance makes him see an opportunity; therefore, his emotion is that of joy.
As we can see, they are three different emotions. The snake, though, remains the same.

What all three reactions have in common is the emotion the person experiences has been unchained by the perception (in the present) that a fact (in the past) modifies our possibilities (in the future).

This is our second concept about emotion dynamics. We hold that an emotion is always the result of an opinion, which is generated by the narrative articulation of the fact we care about.

Then, we reach to a crucial relation for the understanding of the emotional phenomenon: There is a deep relation between our opinions and the emotions we experience.
This is a decisive intuition, given that if it is true, it holds the key that opens the door to distinguish diverse emotions, discover their causes and control them.
And, furthermore, this intuition is the founding block of the bridge we promised to build between reason and passion, since opinions, precisely, are the clearest feature of human rationality.

Facts do not **provoke** emotion, but our particular articulation of them. Facts **initiate** the emotional process, but do not provoke emotion. The emotion we experience is the logical consequence of our **reflection about the facts**, of our own **interpretation** of them. And, there is no doubt said interpretation is the most thorough expression of human reason.

If a person does not know how to cope with the presence of a snake, is it not completely logical to think it is dangerous? Note we are not saying that if you do not know how to cope with the presence of a snake, you should NECESSARILY consider it dangerous. We are only proposing one can consider it so and that would be a logical consequence of one's interpretation.
IF a person sees danger, is it not totally logical and reasonable to feel fear?
On the hand, if someone is used to move around snakes, is it not logical and absolutely reasonable to be cautious not to harm the natural habitat in which the snake lives, thus, trying not to step on the snake?
Finally, if a person likes eating snake meat, is it not completely reasonable to feel joy given then chance to hunt a snake and cook it for dinner that night?

This way, we start to see a feedback circle that explains emotion dynamics:

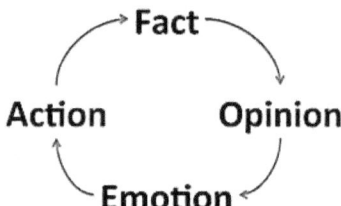

In the first place, we always have a fact. This fact is a state the world is in, which can be the result of the action of external forces (we cannot control them) or the consequence of previous actions we have taken. Here, what really matters is we are talking about verifiable facts, susceptible to be observed. Either they exist, or they do not. They happened, or they did not.

This "state the world is in" provokes us to have a certain opinion. This opinion is conditioned by our own interests and our own mental models. **It is the unavoidable result of our own narrative articulation of those facts.** It is a consequence of our interpretation about them. If we care about something, we will have an opinion about it.

The opinion immediately generates an emotion. This is a key point. WE ARE SAYING THE EMOTION WE FEEL, IS ALWAYS A CONSEQUENCE OF A PERSONAL OPINION. This is the base of emotional rationality. If there is no opinion about the facts, then we will not feel an emotion whatsoever. The fact will continue to exist, but we will not register it. There is nothing in it that matters. We do not care about it.

But, if we have an opinion about such facts, then, we will feel an emotion, UNDOUBTEDLY.

Once we feel the emotion provoked by our opinion, our possibilities for action as a response to it become bounded to the emotional space in which we find ourselves.

Emotions are predisposition for action. In a certain state of mind, some actions are possible for us while others seem impossible.

Then, we take actions. We make our move. The emotion (remember "emouvoir"?) moves us and leads us to act.

Finally, the action modifies the real state, generating new facts. The circle closes and begins once again.

The feedback circle explains that emotion dynamics are easy to understand. However, drawing adequate conclusions and applying it to daily life effectively, is a much harder task. Managing emotions skillfully demands a deep understanding of the explained dynamics, and a constant practice until reaching effectiveness on this domain.

Looking at the figure, the first thing we can say about it is emotions are **NOT** unchained by facts. This is the first big lie we fall into when trying to explain emotions.

Facts do not provoke emotions. It is **OUR** articulation of those facts what founds an opinion and this one, consequently, unchains an emotion.

In order to develop emotional ability, it is necessary to understand this concept deeply. If we believe facts unchain emotions, in order to control emotions, our only chance will be to attempt controlling facts. We should have the power of making facts fit to our desires. In our example, we should be able to make snakes appear and disappear at our will. But, we know this is not possible in real life. We cannot choose whether snakes appear or not. We deal with states the world is in that we cannot manage, that do not submit to our will.

One of the first consequences of ignoring the relation between opinions and emotions is that we try to intervene in emotion dynamics by trying to control facts. But, if we do this, we will fail over and over. It is not within our reach.

Of course, when our attempts of **DIRECTLY** controlling facts fail, our negative emotion will feed itself. Without even realizing about it, failure will provoke negative opinions, which will also feed our emotion (negative as well) even more. In such state, the actions we take will be less effective every time, changing facts (obtained results after taking actions) also in a negative way. We will be worse off. The feedback circle speeds up and becomes completely out of our control. Fury, anger, and deep depression are this process' final stop.

Therefore, we will not achieve effective results on the emotional domain by trying to **DIRECTLY** intervene on facts.

A second alternative (in case we ignore the relation between opinions and emotions) is trying to **DIRECTLY** control the emotion.

For example, when we experience fear, we look to control it by telling ourselves: "I don't have to be scared, I don't have to be afraid."

That attempt to directly intervene on the emotion, **WITHOUT INTERVENING ON THE OPINION THAT UNCHAINS IT**, always ends up being useless. Worse yet, we start trying to suppress the emotion we experience, we deny it, we try to "disconnect" from it. However, the only thing we end up doing is increasing it, since we continue to have it but, now, we consider it illegitimate. We tell ourselves "I am scared, but I shouldn't be. Being afraid is wrong."

The system speeds up and becomes out of our control once again. Panic is the result of being feeling fear, and trying to disconnect from it as the only response.

The only, actually effective, alternative to manage emotions is to **DIRECTLY INTERVENE ON THE OPINION THAT UNCHAINS THEM**.

It is not about trying to make snakes appear or disappear. Or trying to ignore the emotion that the appearance of a snake provokes.

Emotional ability lies in being able to distinguish the unchained emotion, analyze it, find its arguments and, finally, modify such opinion to change to emotion we feel.

**Emotional Ability**

Now we have reached this point, it is time to explore the steps that let us manage emotions.
First step: Distinguishing the emotion
It is important to distinguish the emotion, given that the emotional space is full of possible emotions, many of the quite similar.
Lets suppose we are driving our car, heading to an important date. Suddenly, a tire pops, so we cannot keep going.
First, we will be angry. If we are not skillful in emotional management, we will get angry with the tire, or its maker, or with our "bad luck".
Anger is the result of the opinion "what just happened is bad for me, and, BESIDES, unfair."
Acting with emotional ability, we quickly distinguish we have anger. The key in this first step is, precisely, to realize we "have anger", which is completely different to "being angry".
While having anger as a consequence of something that affects our plans is logic, being angry assumes the emotion has overwhelmed us. "Having anger" implies we have it, that we are still in command. "Being angry" assumes the emotion is in command.
The step of distinguishing the emotion is crucial to stay in touch with it, in order to move on to the second step.
The question we should immediately ask ourselves is: "which emotion am I experiencing?"

Second step: Distinguishing the unchaining opinion from the emotion we are experiencing
Sticking with our anger example, we see that the phrase describing what happens in our minds when we notice the tire has popped has two opinions.
"What just happened (fact- the tire has popped) is BAD for me, and, besides, UNFAIR."
As we said before, the fact the tire has popped does NOT provoke our anger, but the opinion it generates, does. Bad or unfair are opinions. And, sticking with our culture's common sense, they are negative opinions.

Therefore, the emotions these opinions unchain are also negative.

Note the strict rational logic of emotions. If I think something is bad and unfair, it is logical and rational that the emotion I experience as a consequence will be negative.

Anger, then, is the narrative articulation influenced by two negative opinions.

"What happened, or is happening, is bad for me, and, besides, unfair."

This second step in emotion management allows distinguishing the opinion provoking it.

Every emotion is provoked by opinions. If there is no opinion (which is ALWAYS prior to emotion), there will be no emotion.

Of course the celerity with which the opinion impregnates in our minds and unchains the emotion is much greater than how long we try to explain it. It happens with an explosive immediacy. That is why it is so difficult noticing the process and controlling it.

Once we have been "taken" by the emotion, which has overwhelmed us, it will be very complex to clear our mind and distinguish the opinion that generated it.

Here, it is more evident what we said regarding the first step (distinguishing the emotion).

If the opinion we have is "what is happening is bad for me" without adding the opinion of being unfair, we will not have anger. On this case, the emotion is sadness or pity, but not anger. In order to experience anger, we ought to have the opinion it is also unfair.

Third step: working with the unchaining opinion

Working with an opinion means to put our intellect in action.

We have to explore the nature of the opinion and its arguments.

Every opinion either is grounded or ungrounded, and they all provoke emotions. However, being able to notice whether the opinion generating the emotion is grounded or not will be vital to control it. The "emotion strategy" completely changes if we face an emotion provoked by an opinion with arguments, in regards to facing an ungrounded opinion.

If the unchaining opinion is grounded, we will take certain actions. If the opinion is ungrounded, and we are aware of it, when we get to that understanding, the emotion will vanish, and we will stop feeling it.
Then, lets review the characteristics of a grounded opinion:

1) It is inspired by a certain interest.
In order to be grounded, an opinion has to be generated by the influence of a certain interest.
The first question we should be able to answer is: Which is/are the personal interest that is affected by this situation?
Only if we can clearly distinguish the personal interest that is being affected, we will be able to move on to the second step.
2) It has to be backed by facts.
The second question must be: Which is/are the fact that affects my interests?
Here, it is crucial to make a description of the facts BASED ON OBSERVATIONS. Ergo, true or false elements. Facts, not opinions. A grounded opinion is backed by FACTS, not in other opinions. And, those facts must have happened (or be happening) effectively.
3) It refers to a certain action domain.
A grounded opinion does not refer to "generalized reality", it is bounded to a certain action domain.
The question we ought to ask ourselves to clarify the opinion's reference domain is: Which is/are the previous commitments, or plans, that is affected by the existence of these facts?
What we explore here is in what way the facts that provoke the opinion, affect the interests we have and are related with personal plans or commitments. Precisely determining which are the affected interests or commitments turns out being decisive to face the actions that will really be effective in order to overcome the challenge set by circumstances.

When working with the opinion that unchains anger, for example, it is possible that:
a) We discover the opinion that provokes the emotion is UNFOUNDED. On this case, along with the conviction of the lack of arguments for the opinion, the emotion gradually fades away. In the example about anger, this emotion will disappear

if, after exploring the arguments of the opinions that unchain it (bad and unfair), we reach to the conclusion it was not founded to affirm such facts were bad. It is logical to think if we abandon the opinion the facts are bad for me, we will no longer feel anger (even we might still think they are "unfair"). We will say they are unfair (that is, "we do not deserve it") but given we do not consider them bad, it is possible (most of the time) that we no longer care they are unfair.
b) We reach to the conclusion there are arguments to say the facts are bad for me, but, instead, we cannot argue they are unfair. On this case, anger goes away, making room for sadness or pity, emotions that respond to the articulation "what has happened/ is happening is bad for me".
c) We understand that bad and unfair are grounded opinions on this case. Therefore, we have found the causes of our anger, so we can stay in touch with it and be prepared to intervene.

Working with the emotion, clarifying it, finding the arguments that hold the opinion generating it, is crucial to design the actions we will take to intervene. The actions we take to intervene on anger are different to the ones we take to face sadness or pity.

Fourth step: Intervening on the emotion
When we reach this point, we:
a) Have clearly distinguished which is the emotion we are experiencing
b) Have perfectly articulated the opinion that unchains it
c) Have determined our personal interests that are in stake
d) Know without a doubt which facts generated the opinion that unchained the emotion (that means we know the causes of our emotion)
e) Have in clear the plans or commitments affected

At this moment, we unfold the logic of the emotion. We understand it is absolutely rational that, given the interests in stake, the facts that happened and the plans affected, we experience the emotion we are feeling.
We have stayed in touch with our emotion, so it is time to intervene on it.

All we have to do now is taking corrective actions. **BUT SUCH ACTIONS ARE NOT EXERCISED ON THE EMOTION.** It is not about ignoring, suppressing or denying it.
It is about acting on the causes of the emotion; ergo, the facts that generated the opinion, which unchained the emotion.
Working on the causes means analyzing what actions we can take in order to make these causes disappear, or to limit the consequences of the facts, or to look for help from other people we think are competent in the domain of our affected plants or commitments.
The most important, most striking element on this process, is that only by starting it, only by initiating the rational effort to understand what is happening and the emotion this provokes, is enough to begin controlling the emotion.
When working with our emotion, with its causes (unchaining opinion) and with its consequences (actions the emotion predisposes us to), we begin operating at a higher consciousness level, avoiding reacting simply to facts and achieving to deeply review the position we take when we face them, to act with higher effectiveness.
Emotional ability does not imply annulling the emotion, or suppressing or denying it. Quite opposite, it means to put the emotion to our service, not vice versa. It means working with emotion to avoid being at its will and, conversely, making it push us to effective actions.

Once again, every emotion is linked to an opinion. The emotion is the first answer we give, as human beings, when facts happen. It is the most immediate action, previous to any other, an individual generates in the face of a certain fact, or event that catches his attention.

**Emotion language**

Our language provides us a very effective method to manage emotions. The articulation of opinions that generate emotions can be analyzed on the base of a set of steps that, if correctly completed, let us successfully intervene on our personal emotions as much as on other people's.

Even though it is absolutely effective to claim there is a deep relation between language and emotions, such relation is not obvious. It needs to be explained. It is necessary to prove it exists, and making clear which are the relation that determine such influence.

The great advantage in understanding this relation is we are capable of comprehending a domain as a function of another. That is, using our language to articulate an explanation of what happens, we can successfully intervene on what we are experiencing.

When an event, a fact, calls for our attention, we immediately generate an explanation of it (we articulate a "story"). Intervening in that story, we can modify the emotion we experience.

Starting to explain our Emotional Ability method, lets remember an emotion is always generated by thoughts underlying it. The emotion rises as an answer to some phenomenon or event that in a certain situation stands out from the environment. It is guided by reason and intellect.

When incorporating a situation into our intellect, we choose to highlight something we care about, something concerning us. And, we care about it based on the type of observer we are at the time the event happens and we choose to stand it out amongst a great variety of events that are happening simultaneously.

We need to point out different facts happen all the time but our attention is only caught by a few. By those that, for a particular reason, we care about. And, we care about them due to the kind of observer we are at the time, based on articulation about past facts, and because we move towards a certain future. And, this triple, temporal structure where present, past and future converge, gives sense to our emotions.

Regarding this matter about the presence of past, present an future in the generation of emotions, there is a beautiful distinction in Robert Pirsig's "Zen and the Art of Motorcycle Maintenance". It refers to the way we think about time. Generally, when constructing an image of our own position before the facts becoming throughout time, we are used to

imagining an individual standing on his present, observing the future that extends in front of him, while he leaves his past behind. It almost seems like to be looking to shed light on what is about to happen, almost guessing it; in a way we get ahead of facts to respond effectively before them.
Greek, said Pirsig, had quite a different vision of the becoming of time. They imagined a person standing on his present, looking at his past **extending and getting away** from him, while his future advanced, unbeknown and mysterious, **on his back**. Our Greek ancestors did not see the future ahead, but **behind us**. This Greek metaphor of time is much more promising to understand the phenomenon of opinions and emotions. We cannot see the future, given it has not happened yet. We can only imagine it, articulate it, based on our past experiences, influenced by our own present interests. We care about what happens because it responds to interests we have at certain times, and we choose how to take care of them based on our previous experiences, looking for a future that is both uncertain, and deeply important, so we want to act upon it.

If, as we said before, every emotion is generated by our own thoughts, what we have to do is "reconstructing" those thoughts in a way they help us modify the emotion we experience (or, if it is about modifying other people's emotions, helping them to "reconstruct" their own thoughts in a way they achieve modifying the emotions they experience).
Our thoughts are nothing but a conversation we have with "ourselves". To think is to talk silently with oneself. Therefore, if we want to explore the thoughts underlying an emotion, we have to "listen" carefully to each personal, private conversation.

This exploration is an emotional ability that let us inaugurate two action domains. On the first place, we will be able to observe rigorously the opinions that unchain a certain emotion, looking to understand, deeply, the arguments of said opinion and the existing feedback process. Secondly, we will be capable of intervening on those opinions with the objective of modifying them and, in that way, transform the emotions linked to them. The first necessary step, I believe, is unraveling the explanation underlying the emotion. Every emotion is backed by a story, a particular narration expressing an opinion of what happened and can happen in the future.

The first step of our method, then, will be to check the explanation.

This explanation can be referred to the facticity of the world (facts that happened) as well as to possibilities (what can happen or could have happened). The unchained emotion will depend on one or the other.

Secondly, we have to determine the feedback process that, generally, starts working after an emotion is unchained. This circle can be negative or positive, but it is always convenient to visualize it.

It is helpful to clarify emotional ability requires two opposite ways of operating. On one hand, we need to unconditionally accept the emotion that is unchained as a result of our opinion. The feedback process is automatic and begins immediately, despite our choice or immediate possibilities for intervention. We need to accept the emotion as it appears. A very common mistake, sometimes fatal, is trying to stop this process, denying it or criticizing it. Consequences range from modest anger and irritation to alienation and schizophrenia.

Further, it is necessary to analyze rigorously the origin of the emotion, exploring the opinion that unchains it and the room for possibilities for intervention that opens before each of the emotions we experience. Here lies the supposed contradiction, given that, on one hand, we say we have to accept the emotion as it presents, but on the other hand, se claim we have to try intervening on it.

This dilemma is dissolved when we move on to the third step of our method: analyzing the possible room for intervention, which is the exploration of the actions leading us to successfully intervene on the emotion, without denying or suppressing it, but understanding and modifying it.

This step consists of a set of questions we can ask ourselves, or others, which are very useful when exploring the causes of the emotion.

In order to illustrate and teach our method, lets take the example of how to use it to intervene on some of the most common emotions.

**Sadness**
1- Checking the explanation
The explanation that unchains the emotion we call sadness, is:

"What happened means a loss for me."

It is an opinion based on facticity; ergo, facts that happened or are happening.
These facts can be, for example, the demise of a loved one, losing a job, or not accomplishing an objective.

2- Feedback process
When experiencing sadness and not intervening effectively on it, it is likely a negative feedback circle is generated, starting with the refusal of facts. Following with the denial for possibilities in the future that unchains resignation.
When we become resigned, we stop believing in any possibilities to move on. At this point, not only we have the original loss, but also we add the loss of possibilities. The result is a deeper sadness. If we do not intervene adequately, we can fall in a deep depression.

3- Possible room for intervention
Accepting facts. Accepting does not mean we like them. Surely, if we were given the chance to choose, we would opt they did not happen. But, they have happened and it makes no sense to deny that reality. What we can do is checking the facts and actions taken as a response to those facts. Learning from the past.
Allowing oneself to experience pity, gives the chance to assume our loss, accepting the facts and recover the initial harmony. This way, it is possible to say goodbye to what we loved, understanding its ephemeral, contingent and limited condition in time. That way, we incorporate this experience to our own story, accepting, unconditionally, what happened as

contingency in our lives. We add, then, the learning that took place, opening new possibilities for us.

When taking these actions we understand pain as transitory, while we perceive the values leading us to love what we love, as permanent. We understand we can love someone who is gone. This generates new confidence in ourselves, given we realize that even when certain circumstances can cause pain for our loss, we know how to respond to the challenge pain implies.

This increase of self-confidence allows us to assume the risks of living a contingent life once more.

If, conversely, we suppress sadness, we also have to suppress the love for who/what we loved. We become stoic and less humane. Transitory pain becomes permanent suffering. We cling to who/what we loved and me refuse its end. We do not see the limited temporality or contingency in our lives. We fall into resentment (denying facts) and later on into negative resignation (refusal of possibilities). Fearful of ongoing suffering, and admitting incompetent to face pain, we shut our heart to the possibility of wanting something new. We do not have the capacity to assume the risks of living exploring new action alternatives. We fall into despair and unhappiness.

The questions that can help us to intervene successfully on sadness are:

What is the fact that makes me sad?
What is the loss I experienced?
What are the facts leading me to think I lost it?
What is the value that I give to what I lost?
Is it possible to take an action to get it back?
Is it possible to take an action to reduce the negative consequences of this loss?
Is there someone who can help me minimize this loss?

**Happiness**

1- Checking the explanation

The explanation that unchains the emotion we call happiness, is:

"What happened is good for me."

It is an opinion based on facticity; ergo, facts that have happened or are happening.
These facts can be, for example, achieving an objective, the birth of someone we love, or getting a job.

2- Feedback process
Happiness is based on facticity (facts) of life. It implies the acceptance of new possibilities. Up to here, the feedback circle is positive given the result is enthusiasm, the engine for many productive actions.
But, we need to be careful as, from then on, new possibilities are perceived as facts, like results we already got, so we fall into an excess of confidence that leads to a state of euphoria, which ignores the voice of prudence. This way, we are no longer enthusiasts but reckless. And, we will be exposed to great failures.

3- Possible room for intervention
Celebrating the achievement. The celebration marks a milestone, a moment to check actions. It helps to be aware of the travelled path and the one we have to walk as well. The celebration of a certain achievement helps not to fall into the unfounded euphoria.
Allowing oneself to experience happiness, lets being cognizant about the moment, reminding the effort made to achieve the objective and appreciate the aid we received.
When freely experiencing happiness, we become more thankful, and appreciation always predisposes for humbleness. When we joyfully celebrate our existence, we can accept contingent events throughout our lives. Celebrating implies acknowledging the obtained achievement could have not happened. When we live happiness fully, we remember that winning and losing are part of living. Even when we have made our biggest effort, we never have the certainty of granted success. And, we become happy and celebrate precisely because we acknowledge it.
If, contrarily, we suppress happiness, we lose the opportunity of accepting our achievements, and we become stoic. Then, we fall into the illusion that the achievement obtained is the "logic and inevitable consequence of our actions." We forget

contingency that exists in our lives. We fall into the trap of believing success is a **direct** consequence of our actions, every time we succeed. We begin living our achievements as "natural". Nothing moves us.
When we do not celebrate we let go the opportunity to mark a milestone and get prepared for the future.
The questions that can help us intervene successfully on happiness are:
What is the fact that makes me happy?
What is the benefit I experienced?
What did I get?
Which is the value I give to what I got?
How should I celebrate the obtained result?
Is there anyone I can thank for helping me achieve my goal?

**Fear**
1- Checking the explanation
The explanation that unchains the emotion we call fear, is:

"What is about to happen (or might have happened but is not confirmed yet) is bad for me."

It is about an opinion based on contingency (possible events, but not inevitable).
These events can be, for example, noticing the chance that I have not studied enough for my exam, getting bad news about an accident that happened near where family and friends live and supposing they could be hurt.

2- Feedback process
Fear encourages protecting either oneself or others. When fear overwhelms, it provokes inaction, due to the refusal of taking any risks. It turns into panic, which leads to total immobility.

3- Possible room for intervention
Protecting what is valuable, and exploring the foundation of the double opinion generated by fear (the opinion that something can happen and the opinion that would be bad). Backing on observations about facts to analyze the possibility there are other facts that can support an opposite opinion.

Checking standards and expectations to find out whether they can be changed for others that make fear diminish or disappear. Analyzing if there are actions that can avoid what is bad from happening, or, if it happens, that the results do not be drastic. If we lack the competence to take such actions, asking help from those who have those abilities.

When intervening on our fear, we retake our place of responsibility before events throughout life. We allow ourselves to experience fear, to be in touch with it, helping us understand the risk of losing what we value is part of life. The only way not to fear is by not desiring anything.

When allowing fear to flow, we can use it in our favor, taking advantage of the advices given by fear's positive branch: prudence.

If, contrarily, we do not let ourselves experience fear, we face two great dangers.

First, we might silence the voice of prudence. Being afraid when there are grounded reasons for it, it is not an act of pusillanimity, but of conscience and wisdom. Only those who overestimate their own competence do not experience fear.

Second, suppressed fear can explode one day. When we have ignored our fears for a long time, they can abruptly irrupt, turned into panic. On this case, the most probable consequence is immobility. Fear will have grown so much it will not be able to be controlled in our favor. We lose the possibility to respond to events, and we turn into victims of our fear.

The questions that can help us intervene successfully on fear are:

What am I afraid of?
What I do think could happen?
What are the negative consequences I should face if that happens?
What makes me think that is likely to happen?
What makes me think that I will be hurt it that happens?
Is there something I can do to avoid that from happening?
Is there any action I could take to reduce the probability that it happens?
Is there any action I could take in order to reduce the damage I will suffer if it happens?
Is there anyone I can seek to help me out if it happens?

**Enthusiasm**
1- Checking the explanation
The explanation that unchains the emotion we call enthusiasm, is:

"What is about to happen (or already happened but is not confirmed yet) is good for me."

It is about an opinion based on contingency (possible events, but not inevitable).
These events could be, for example, imagining a new project, making plans, opening a conversation with an important, possible client, waiting for a positive answer to a love declaration.

2- Feedback process
Enthusiasm promotes the visualization of new opportunities. When these opportunities are not supported by precise competence, or facts backing them up, enthusiasm drifts onto inveterate optimism, leading us to interpret as opportunities even those situations we have no chance of intervening positively or effectively. The unfounded optimism predisposes us to take extreme risks.

3- Possible room for intervention
Channeling enthusiasm through concrete and effective actions. Restricting the domain of those actions to the range of grounded possibilities for intervention, given the current competence. Taking advantage of the opportunities to learn new abilities that open new possibilities.
Contrasting personal expectations with potential opportunities, trying to rigorously argue that they are, effectively, possibilities in our reach.
Focusing the enthusiasm on actions that respond to those potential possibilities.
When we take care of our enthusiasm, we get a great energy. We become proactive and generate actions. Results aside, we experience the integrity of living in a constant pursuit to generate value for us, and those around us.

This way, we live the experience of unconditional integrity, given our enthusiasm does not depend on the result (always contingent) of our actions, but of having explored completely the possibilities we foresee in life, taking the actions matching with them.

If, for any reason, we suppress enthusiasm, we deny opportunities and possibilities. Fearing not to succeed, we prefer to ignore or deny such opportunities exist. Nothing "is for us". We take a cynical position and we hopelessly fall into a negative resignation, leading to resentment.

The questions that can help us successfully intervene on enthusiasm are:
What enthusiasts me?
What are the possibilities that open up if it happens?
How likely is that to happen?
What are the reasons to wish it happens?
How would the world look like if I get it what I wish for?
Which concrete actions that I currently cannot take, could I take if it happens?
Is there anyone who has actively participated so that happens or has chances of happening?

**Four basic emotional states in a human being's life**

An emotional state is the result of an emotion that is kept for a long term. While the emotion responds to a conjuncture, being volatile, an emotional state is more permanent.

Throughout our lives, there are four states of mind we can call "basic", given how often many people experience them. Lets explore them together.

We have said that we generate explanations of certain events we face and care about. When articulating this explanation, the individual makes sure to distinguish the components of the situation to be faced. He tries to identify the causes of what happened, and the future consequences he guesses will come. All this process, we have also said, is based on our capacity to express opinions. A certain domain in which we are capable of

expressing opinions is the Domain of Facticity and Possibilities Judgment.
Additionally, we have seen emotions can be originated in opinions coming from facts or perception of possibilities. It is time to join such intuitions.

When observing a certain situation, we immediately try characterizing it, putting it in some comprehension category to make it easier its incorporation and understanding.
The first category we usually use is the one defining the area of what we consider invariable, immutable, not open to change. We will call this category the Domain of Facticity.
Further, there is another category that feeds from what is susceptible to change, open to be modified. We will call this category the Domain of Possibilities.

**Domain of Facticity**
In our lives, there is a space not open to change. No matter what we do, how we act, the state of matters will not change; the conditions will continue to be the same.
The clearest example is one related to our biology. We cannot operate further the limits our body has. There are "colors" we cannot see, "sounds" we cannot hear, and of course, certain abilities we cannot perform, like flying with no external help.
Some of this limitations stick with us through our entire lives, while others are a bit more temporary. There are specific moments in a lifetime in which we are capable of performing certain actions we cannot perform in other circumstances. It is a certainty that at each moment in our lives we are limited by our biological conditions. It is a facticity, for example, that we will not become tennis stars at the age of 90, no matter how much we try and train (which will not be much at that age either).

A second type of facticity is the one referring to the past. Those facts that already happened and we cannot modify. We were born in the place we did, we had the parents we had, and we have done whatever we have done. All these facts, whether we like them or not, cannot be modified.

Finally, we have the facticity related to the historic moment we live in. At each moment in history, there are things impossible to change. For example, for the people living during the second decade of the XXI Century, it is impossible to live in Saturn. We cannot assure this will not change in the future, but we are absolutely sure it is impossible at the time being.

However, there is a subtle difference between this type of facticity and the two previous ones. While the first two are composed by facts, the last one introduces us in the domain of possibilities judgment. The first two will never be modifiable, whatever happens. Historic facticity tells us there are things that are not possible currently, but it does not talk about tomorrow.

Nonetheless, even though they can be modified in the future, the historical context conditions are factual at each moment.

**Domain of Possibilities Judgment**

Just like there are situations we cannot modify, there are others we can.

Every time we refer to a possibility, we are expressing an opinion. The capacity we have to base our opinions of possibilities determines in a decisive way what are the objectives we will be able to reach.

According to Savater, happiness is the nonconformist's wish. Thanks to this nonconformity, we grow every day. Its roots can be found in our capacity to express an opinion, to judge everything can be better, and that we can do many things to make it happen.

Precisely, the opinions we have about our own possibilities are what inspire us (or do not), what make us dream, and make those dreams come true. And, as humane as we are, once we have turn such dreams into reality, new opinions of possibilities form in our head, taking us to try everything again.

We express opinions when we decide we can have a partner, or form a family, or have children, or study a major, or start a company.

Perhaps, the greatest possibilities judgment we can make is about love. When we love, we see ourselves in a better place; the person we love opens possibilities never imagined before. Loving is feeling everything is possible. Mark Twain describes it nicely on "Diaries of Adam and Eve", when Adam writes Eve the epitaph: "Wherever she was, that was Paradise."

**What attitudes can we take before facts and possibilities?**

Before any situation life presents, facing any challenge, it is possible to distinguish what belongs to facticity and what seems possible.

This first step to design a state of mind to live in and develop is not an easy one. It is about drawing a "dividing line" between FACTS and POSSIBILITIES.

| FACTS | POSSIBILITIES |
|---|---|
|  |  |

If we draw this line "too close to the left side" we will be making the mistake of considering something you cannot modify as it were a possibility, given it belongs to the realm of facts. We will make efforts in vain, trying to change something immutable. Due to this fatal error, we can experience a great deal of anguish and ineffectiveness.

But, if we draw the line "too close to the right side", we will be interpreting situations that can be changed as immutable facts. The result is a painful loss of power, and the unhappiness it provokes.

Then, drawing this "dividing line" with expertise is a crucial ability for personal development.

However, even though it is hard, it is just the first step. Now, we have to decide what attitude to take facing facts and possibilities.

Once again, there are two options we can choose from: rejecting or accepting.

This way, we have a more complex table where we must "put" each of the basic states of mind.

|  | Facts | Possibilities |
|---|---|---|
| Reject |  |  |
| Accept |  |  |

Rejecting facts means taking the position of not accepting what happened. It is not about the facts' "denial". It is about rejecting them and desperately looking someone to blame, knowing they have happened. We strongly resent the old facts and we do not generate new ones. We become victims of immobility. Usually, the search for guilty (people) or guiltiness ("society" or "circumstances") is the first reaction we have before a situation that is harmful. Someone or something out there must be guilty.

The attitude of rejecting facts, not accepting them, takes us to RESENTMENT.

|  | Facts | Possibilities |
|---|---|---|
| Reject | RESENTMENT |  |
| Accept |  |  |

On 1817, in England, Mary Shelley published what is considered the first science fiction novel in history. "Frankenstein; or The Modern Prometheus". The book explores science ethics, the morals of the time, the limits of medicine and the relation between men and God. But, we can also say the main topic is resentment. The creature Doctor Viktor Frankenstein brings to life incessantly looks for human approval. The entire first part of the book tells his desperate search for a place amongst men, and his attempts to be a part of the human community.

However, his body provokes rejection and fear. All of his attempts fail. Then, the creature turns into a monster. He cannot accept that rejection and starts looking for someone to blame for his misery. And, when he thinks he has found them, he kills them. Resentment takes him to murder and resignation of not being able to change his condition; it takes him to admit his final goal: destroying his creator. Resentment explains the

genesis and fate of one of the most feared monsters in history of literature.
The path to resentment begins by declaring what happened should not have happened, that it is unfair. And that someone has to pay for it. When looking for revenge, we become more sinister, obsessed to make someone pay for our pain.

It is important to understand we are not suggesting that the search for justice is a negative attitude. Precisely, the key is to seek for justice, not revenge. Seeking for justice is completely opposite to revenge. Making sure that fairness prevails implies, in the first place, accepting facts and, then, to explore what happened, with the final goal that everyone takes responsibility for their actions.

Jean Valjean is, in my opinion, one of the greatest characters in classic literature. A man, tortured and tormented, but kind and magnanimous at the same time, created by Victor Hugo, becomes the light showing the world some of the deepest human reflections.
It is not strange Valjean has something to say about vengeance and justice.
Confined in his cell in Tolon, dressed in his red coat with a 24601 that had replaced his own name, Jean Valjean begins to wonder about his fate. At that moment in his life, he might still be ignorant, but far from being a fool. He thinks, reflects. And he judges himself.
Creating a court of his own within the limits of his conscience, Valjean understands he is not at all an innocent man suffering an unfair punishment. He has stolen, which is a felony, and he knows is. He did it, also true, because he was hungry and because he needed to find clothes for his sister, as well as to feed her and his seven nieces and nephews. However, this does not justify it. Jean Valjean acknowledges his actions have been extreme and dishonorable. He realizes it is possible had he asked for the stolen bread instead, they would not have denied it to him. He sees he should have been patient, even when hunger was pushing him over the edge. That, in the end, one can always wait for help, given it is exceptionally rare for someone to literally starve to death. That, choosing patience

would have been better for him and the children. That it is a ridiculous and shameful to think stealing is the way out of misery. That felony only leads to infamy.
Jean Valjean thinks this while in prison, in Tolon.
But, he also questions himself if he was the only one to have acted wrongly. He reflects about the punishment he was getting. He asks himself whether a disproportional punishment ends up creating confusion. If, once the felony is accepted and confessed, excessive retaliation accounted by the law does not become in abuse.
Within these contrasting thoughts, marvelously put, vengeance and justice are exposed. The responsibility of admitting facts, and the excess that ends up crossing them. The rest of *Les Miserables* fundamentally revolves around these ruminations. Perhaps, that is why this play's legacy is unforgettable and indispensable.

It is possible we may have a perfectly grounded our guiltiness judgment. But, if based on that judgment all we do is to seek to "make someone pay the price", trying to inflict pain on whoever is guilty, we will be stuck in the situation.
Revenge, which is resentment's dearest daughter, blinds us. Our conscience is filled with the desire of hurting whomever we consider guilty for our pain. We reject any other possibility. We fall into resignation.

|        | Facts      | Possibilities |
|--------|------------|---------------|
| Reject | RESENTMENT | RESIGNATION   |
| Accept |            |               |

Resignation is a prostration kind of state of mind. To resign is to give up, to stop wishing and dreaming. It is to sentence future's death.
But, there is a moment we need to rise up. To accept what happened and try moving forward. Accepting and assimilating facts that constitute our life. We cannot choose whether they have happened. But, there they are, taking part of our past. We have to assimilate them and make them part of our future.

Accepting those facts, even though they make us generate quite negative opinions, will allow us to quit looking for someone to blame and put us in conditions to generate actions aiming towards the future.
To look at our future, we need to be at peace with our past.

|        | Facts      | Possibilities |
|--------|------------|---------------|
| Reject | RESENTMENT | RESIGNATION   |
| Accept | PEACE      |               |

When we accept the facts and assimilate them to our future, we are at peace with everyone else and ourselves. Whatever facts compose our past and present, we are willing to make them part of our lives, to embrace them, and live with them.
Our experience is composed by successes and failures, joy and sadness. Pleasure and suffering, the two elements that blend in our mix. But, besides nostalgia and luck, we are alive. But, that is not permanent. We have the moral obligation of seizing life.
"Carpe Diem!" as Professor Keating would say.
Or, "Life, we are at peace" as Amado Nervo would declare.

I remember the first time I read that poem. I was at my grandmother's, it was raining outside and the children next door had stopped playing **fútbol** due to this climatic imposition.
My mother was ordering some old paperwork when she found amongst them a notebook she used to read in elementary school.
I can still listen to her reading to me "At Peace" by Amado Nervo.

*Very near my setting sun, I bless you, Life*
*because you never gave me neither unfilled hope*
*nor unfair work, nor undeserved sorrow/pain*

*because I see at the end of my rough way*

*that I was the architect of my own destiny
and if I extracted the sweetness or the bitterness of things
it was because I put the sweetness or the bitterness in them
when I planted rose bushes I always harvested roses*

*Certainly, winter is going to follow my youth
But you didn't tell me that May was eternal
I found without a doubt long my nights of pain
But you didn't promise me only good nights
And in exchange I had some peaceful ones*

*I loved, I was loved, the sun caressed my face*

*Life, you owe me nothing, Life, we are at peace!*

I like to think we should remember this poem every time the day is over. When drowsiness begins to beat us, we should feel the day was seized. That we are at peace.
This way we will be ready for the last step, which projects a nicer future.

|  | Facts | Possibilities |
|---|---|---|
| **Reject** | RESENTMENT | RESIGNATION |
| **Accept** | PEACE | ASPIRATION |

Life consists of so much more than just checking goals off the bucket list. Our life is a work of art. And, of course, putting together a work of art requires ability, but it requires ongoing perseverance far more. Facing the world, accepting the possibilities that present to us. Because, like Serrat says:

*Sometimes, life
Drinks a coffee with me.
And she is so pretty it is nice to see her.
She loosens her hair and calls me
To go out there with her.*

Based on the state of mind we call ASPIRATION we can make our life a permanent commitment to the generation of material wealth and spiritual richness.

That way, we can relive that beautiful, imposing, challenging commitment a set of American poets made when the XVIII Century was coming to an end. Commitment to unite emotion and rationality. Building a bridge between rationality and passion.

It is impossible to have emotions if we do not have a moral, a set of values expressing the best of our life choices. And those choices are the product of our rationality. But, it is also impossible to be rational lacking emotional preferences. Like Albert Camus expressed with the main character on his novel, "The Stranger". He was someone who lacked emotions; therefore, a moral. He was someone who felt nothing for anything. He was someone who, being incompetent to experience emotions, was not able to discern between good and evil, beautiful and abject. And he ends his life turned into a murderer, simply because he "felt nothing".

Every emotion is backed on some sort of interest, something we care about. And we know every interest responds to logic, to a choice of priorities.

Giving in to love is giving in to reason. And vice versa. We love what we care about. And, when deciding what is it we care about, logic and reason rule.

I hope we can all understand it. To reunite reason and emotions. The same way a poet uses his intellect to express the words that move us.

Only like that, as my master Rafael Echeverría used to say, we will be ready and prepared for the great task we have ahead of us: **Preparing the poets' victorious return.**

# Chapter 4
## At least, that is my point of view

Although quite some time went by, I still remember that billboard. A white man, blandishing a truncheon, runs behind another man. This second man is black, and younger than the one behind him. He seems to be screaming and reaches his right arm forward, as if asking for something. The caption below the picture reads: ANOTHER PROOF OF INTOLERANCE?

The billboard was displayed all over London for a week. Streets, underground stations, bus stops showed the scene. Everyone assumed it was about a campaign against discrimination. Everyone was sure about understanding the message: The white man was running behind the black one to hit him. Probably, the black man was protesting for his people's rights, and the white man was someone with opposite ideas to peaceful coexistence.

But, a week later, another billboard appeared. The picture kept showing the same two men, at mass, with the same attitude. The only difference was the picture was more panoramic and included more actors. Now, one could see both men were behind a third one. This last man had a woman's purse, which he obviously had stolen seconds before.

Both men on the first billboard were police officers. The scene was a real one, pictured by a security camera during it. This time, the billboard, part of a London Police campaign, read a different caption: OR ANOTHER PROOF OF YOUR INTOLERANCE?

Fewer times have I seen the concept of mental models used more accurately than on this campaign. The idea of, first, showing one part of the scene, leaving room for the interpretation of the citizens, so then the complete scene could be exposed, collapsing mostly everyone's expectations, still amazes me.

On the first mental model, the black man was escaping from the white man's violence. In many cultures, this is what we are used to see. And this custom, influences enormously on the articulation of the scene the first picture showed.

What makes this extraordinary is the caption of the second billboard. When saying, "another proof of YOUR intolerance", it clearly establishes intolerance lies within the observer, not within the white man running behind the black man. If the vast majority "saw" a white man chasing a black one, this vision (proved inaccurate on the second billboard) came from the observer's prejudice, from his mental models, and NOT from the picture of the scene. The fact that almost nobody thought both men were working together towards the same objective (on this case, capturing the thief), showed clearly the set of assumptions and beliefs prevailing in the community.

Assumptions and beliefs. The key aspect in mental models.
One time, having a conversation with my friend Peter Senge (author of "The Fifth Discipline", chosen as one of the top twenty management books of the XX Century), I had the chance of listening to one of the two most effective, in my opinion, definitions of mental models.
Peter holds mental models are "a set of assumptions and beliefs deeply ingrained, never questioned, determining how we see the world and how we take actions in it."
The definition begins by explaining what define our mental models are those assumptions, whatever we take "for granted", we never check. The power of mental models lies, precisely, on the fact we never check them. We take those assumptions as the base of out thinking, but we never remember they are assumptions. We tell ourselves "that's just the way it is", and we never review this statement.
Once we have taken these assumptions, **our** assumptions, as the "obvious and real" way to look at the world, it is absolutely logical we act according to this vision. We never ask ourselves about the origin of these assumptions.

This takes us to the second definition of mental models I anticipated forming the couple of most effective definitions.
Rafael Echeverría explained this one to me, and it is much shorter than Senge's, but equally as powerful.
Mental models, says Rafael, are "the moment at which our questioning stops."
The sentence is compelling. It highlights, and reminds us, there always is a moment at which we stop making (ourselves) questions. Our capacity of inquiring and doubting always has a limit and, at a certain point, we cease questioning. Precisely what is left out of question composes what we call mental models.

The best example to illustrate this concept takes me back to my years as a student in elementary school.

Our teacher was explaining the events that lead to Columbus first voyage to "India". She was telling us how brave the Genoese sailor had been by deciding a voyage assuming the world was round, hence making it possible to reach "India" by sailing west.

Our teacher added Columbus had to convince the people financing the voyage that the established idea of the world's shape was in fact wrong.

The teacher showed us a cardboard illustrating the beliefs of the XV Century: the drawing pictured a flat world, supported by four giant elephants, which were standing over the shell of an enormous turtle.

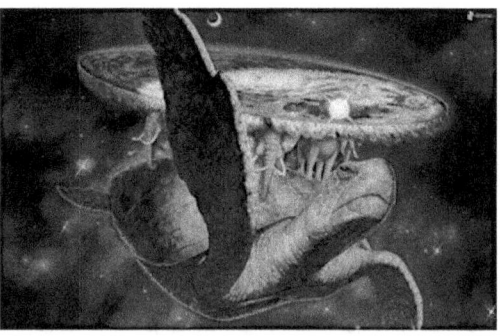

I remember the surprise followed by the laughter that cardboard caused us. We could not believe "grown ups" could believe such an explanation.

Quickly, we began asking our teacher some questions:

Where did the people think the water falling from the flat world go?

What did the elephants and turtle eat?

Who fed them?

Why would the elephants stay there, supporting the weight, instead of escaping?
But the most disturbing question was:
Where did the turtle stand?

This last question is the example we are looking for. That was the question NOBODY asked. It was not discussed. People did not even think about it.
Lets imagine the dialogue between two people at the beginning of the XV Century:
-What is the world's shape?
-Flat, of course, as we all know.
-So, what is supporting the world?
-Easy, over four giant elephants.
-Really? So tell me, where are these four elephants standing?
-Come on man, everyone knows that: over the shell of an enormous turtle.
-Oh, that makes sense now!

This imaginary dialogue is significant because there is someone who questions and someone who answer according to the time's "common sense".
But, as the questions are answered (each of them with answers a human from current times would consider a joke), the questioning begins to cease.
Until they reach to the last explanation, the one with the turtle. And there, instead of asking the question that seems obvious now-a-day (where does the turtle stand?), the one asking the questions stops, stops asking and accepts the "common sense" as the final explanation. And claims he now understands.

The point is the turtle is paradigmatic. It is the foundation of the prevailing mental model of the time. The enormous turtle represents that "set of assumptions and beliefs deeply ingrained, never questioned, which determine how we see the world and how we take actions in it, in Senge`s words, or the "place" at our questioning stops" as Rafael states. There are no questions further the idea of the turtle. The questioning stops there.

I said the drawing had made us, the children, laugh. And, probably, the picture you saw on this book caused you a similar reaction. Then, I propose you to imagine the following conversation, now between two people like you and me, people of the XXI Century, well informed and cultured people.
-What is the world's shape?
-Well, it is a geoid, as we all know.
-And, what supports the world?
-Easy, it is floating within our Galaxia, the Milky Way.
-Really? So, where is the Milky Way floating?
-Come on man, everyone knows that: it's floating on the Universe.
-Oh, that makes sense now!

More than five centuries have let us change the "enormous turtle" for the "Universe". But, there still is a moment at which, for now, our questioning stops. We say the Milky Way is floating on the Universe and express "it makes sense."

I would like to clarify I am not proposing mental models are pernicious, nor we should vanish them.
I am merely stating there **ARE** mental models, we **ALL** have them, and there is much to learn from them.
In the first place, mental models are useful and help us reach effectiveness. Our lives would be impossible if we did not have them. Without these assumptions and beliefs, we would be questioning what we perceive all the time. We would need to permanently organize everything we see, everywhere we go to. We would be confused. We would be inhibited to act. I'd like to illustrate it with a daily routine example.
We all know what an elevator is. We are used to seeing and using them. We distinguish one when we see it. However, not every elevator is the same. There are some old ones, with manual doors, and there are modern ones, with automatic doors. But this does not confuse us. We know how to distinguish them. When we reach a building's lobby and the receptionist tells us to "take the elevator to the eighteenth floor", we take a look and immediately walk towards it. We know how to act and what to wait for, even though it might be

the first time we are at that building. We do not stand there, perplexed, not knowing how to react.

But, imagine for a moment what would happen if we did not have an "elevator" mental model. We would have to learn what is it about every time we had to use a new one.

We would see, for example, two doors that open automatically at the lobby. We would see a group of people enter a little room. We would see the doors closing. We would see some lights turning on and off on a little panel placed right above the doors. And, to our astonishment and horror, minutes later we would see the doors open automatically once again, with nobody inside!

In such circumstances, I doubt we would accept "taking the elevator to the eighteenth floor". Most likely, we would immediately run away.

Having an "elevator" mental model lets us go with effectively, without the need to take the stairs.

Therefore, mental models are quite useful. The problem appears when we forget they are mental models, and we start "being sure" it is just the "way it is". Difficulties rise when we forget they are a set of assumptions, an explanation of how and why things happen. On this case, we completely stop our questioning and fall into the "trap of double forgetting".

Let me explain this trap. The problem does not lie in "having" a mental model. It does not even lie in "forgetting" what we perceive is the result of a mental model. The real problem is "forgetting we have forgotten" we "have" a mental model.

How do we explain this word play?

Once again, we will illustrate it with an example. Everyone who drives a car has a mental model explaining how to drive. Particularly, we all have a mental model on how to make the "car speed up". This is accomplished by stepping on what we call "gas".

Actually, what makes the car increase its speed is a complicated combustion process, which starts with the flow of the fuel through certain parts of the engine. This step can be achieved by "stepping on the gas", but it can also be done by pressing a button, or by pulling a cable.

"Stepping on the gas" is the automatic action, no doubt about it, which rises from the mental model we have about how the car works. Nobody wastes time on reflecting about the "mechanics of internal combustion and complex chemical processes that incite it". When we drive a car, we simply "step on the gas".

This is the moment of the first "forgetting". When stepping on the gas we do not remember the internal combustion process, we do not think about chemical equations. We simply respond to our mental model about how to drive a car and we act upon it. We "forget" it is about a mental model and that "actually, a greater quantity of fuel is feeding the car's internal combustion."

This "first forgetting" is very effective. Life would be unbearable, and very inefficient, if every time we take an action, we reflect about the arguments making it possible. We should permanently check our mental models, question them, test them, draw conclusions, and then, speed up. We would surely cause more troubles than an elephant in a china shop.

When we forget we are dealing with a mental model, we just speed up. We bypass it. And life goes on. And that is a really good thing.

The "first forgetting" consists on "having a mental model" and "forgetting" it is about a mental model. When we do this, we reach the effectiveness of not questioning everything, all the time.

But, what happens if when stepping on the gas the car does not speed up? This is the moment at which we should not become victims of the "second forgetting". It is the moment at which we should remember "stepping on the gas to make the car speed up", responds to a mental model. What provokes the increase in speed IS NOT the action of stepping on the gas, but the internal combustion process.

If we forget this last concept, we will fall into the "trap of double forgetting". We will have forgotten all we had was a mental model. We will "have forgotten we had forgotten" it was a mental model. And all we will try doing is stepping "harder" on the gas, waiting for some "miracle" to happen.

More clearly put:

Step 1: We learn how a process works (on this case we learn a car's "acceleration" depends of a chemical process starting from stepping on the gas).
Step 2: We construct the mental model about the process (given we want to increase the car's speed, we have to "step on the gas").
Step 3: We forget it is a mental model so we do not have to reflect and doubt it every time we use this process.
Step 4: If when "stepping on the gas" the car does not speed up, we remember we had a mental model about how to achieve more speed, but what actually speeds the car up is the chemical process happening inside the car's engine.

If we do not complete Step 4 (ergo, we "forget we had forgotten" we had a mental model about the car's acceleration), we will fall into the trap of double forgetting, and we will only try to step harder on the gas.
If we complete Step 4, we will remember we had forgotten, and we will be able to check the engine's performance, eventually achieving to repair the malfunctioning.

Conclusion: mental models are useful; they help life be more efficient and foreseeable. Danger lies in forgetting they are mental models.

**Maps and Mental Models**

Clearly, we all have a set of assumptions and beliefs deeply ingrained that we never (or almost never) check.
Mental models are present at all times, conditioning experiences as much as their interpretations, and guiding the inferences we make based on the "reality" we perceive.
Somehow, mental models are like maps we use to walk the world, to function day by day.
Just like any map, mental models have an intention; they are never neutral. Far from it being a flaw, intentionality is within the nature of a good map.
A map, in order to be effective, necessarily chooses barely some aspects of the reality it is trying to represent, leaving aside other aspects that are not relevant for the its end.

If maps did not have an "intention", they would be perfectly useless.
Lets say, for example, that I decide to travel by car from Mar del Plata to Bariloche. Further, lets assume I do not know the road. On such circumstances, a good idea would be to get a map. But, is any map good?
Of course not. I need a map representing the southern region of Argentina. But, once again, I ask myself: Is any map of the southern region of Argentina good? Again, the answer is "no". I need a route map of the southern region of Argentina.
It is likely there are other maps of the same region that are more "complete", or prettier, or colorful, or cheaper. But, given my objectives, if the map does not include a precise representation of the routs I need to travel to get to Bariloche from Mar del Plata, it will be completely useless.
Then, I need a map drawn with an intention (an interested map), a representation of reality discarding those characteristics of the territory that are irrelevant for me, given my objectives, specific interests and circumstances. This does not mean other possible maps (zoographic, climatological, or geological) are incorrect. They just do not serve my purpose on this occasion. A very simple map, perhaps a few lines drawn on a piece of paper, with short references, will be more adequate for this moment than the prettiest, most complete water, lacustrine map of the Argentine Patagonia.

When try to understand a situation, when we pretend "making sense" of an experience, we will also need to draw a "map" of "reality". On this case, it is about a mental map. But, just like its paper equal, mental maps are also intended, and respond to certain conjunctural objectives of the individual making them. In order to undertake the practice of human communication is crucial to unconditionally accept each person has a right to generate his own map or mental model.
Additionally, it is indispensable to understand each person will do the best they can, given the mental model they have.

Starting from mental models, our thinking structures are guided by what Chris Argyris, Emeritus Professor from Harvard University, called the "Inference Ladder".

According to Argyris, we live in a world of assumptions we consider self-evident, so we assume it is absolutely unnecessary to check. As a consequence, we construct the following logic chain:

1-My beliefs are not beliefs; they are the truth
2-The truth must be "obvious" to anyone who is "intelligent" and "well intended"
3-This truth is based on facts of reality
4-The facts that I choose describe reality perfectly.

But, it turns out reality is much bigger and richer than we suspect. These qualities make it unabated for our mental models. When acting based on this logic chain, it is necessary to be careful. This logic chain, which we will call "Inference ladder" offers advantages as well as disadvantages.

On one hand, inferences are very useful since they give as a level of indispensable "certainty" to function day by day. We have seen this on the elevator example.
For example, if someone asks us "what time is it?" we answer immediately the time of the place we are at. We automatically infer that the desire of whoever asked the question will be satisfied with that answer. We do not ask ourselves, for example, if the time he pretends to know corresponds to the Greenwich meridian, or Siberia's time (unless, of course, we find ourselves in Greenwich or Siberia at that moment).
On this case, the capacity of inferring gives effectiveness to our actions, saving time and resources.
On the other hand, inferences can turn into a great danger. Many times, they are the origin of unproductivity, misunderstanding, and anguish. A boss that asks his employee to finish a report "as soon as possible" may be inferring that, based on that petition, his employee will leave everything else aside and will exclusively work on finishing the report. But, the employee may infer his boss wants him to finish the report as soon as he finishes with "the great amount of pending tasks, without starting with a new one".

To make things worse, we are used to ignoring we are inferring and we think we are observing concrete facts of "reality". The process of inferring seems so automatic we do it "without realizing it", absolutely sure our interpretation (the one we do not even see as such) is the ONLY LOGICAL AND REASONABLE WAY to understand the situation (do you remember what we said about mental models and the trap of double forgetting?).

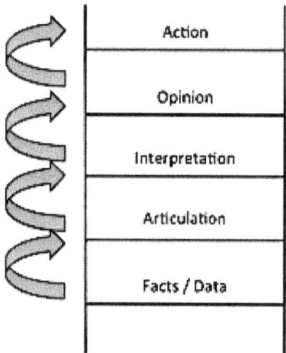

**The inference ladder** is a model describing the way in which we mentally "ascend" from facts to actions.
As we can see on the drawing, the inference ladder shows five "steps". Each of them representing a process most times we do not even know we are going through.

On the first step we find facts, which can be observed. Data our mental models select, from the surrounding reality. We have seen it is about data an observer, committed to certain interests and results, has chosen to distinguish from a much larger observable universe.
The second step is composed by what we will call the articulation of those facts. At this moment, we "mix up" the data, turning them into a congruent and integrated story. As we can see, we do not only choose some data (we do this on the

first step), buy also we "invent" a story when we entwine that data (second step).
Then, lets move on to the third step: interpretations. Here, we design an explanation of what is happening. We try to answer questions like: Why is this happening? What are we looking for? What are the values guiding the actions we are observing? This way, we give meaning to their causes and consequences. These interpretations will be decisive to move to the two last steps on our ladder.
Then, we reach to the fourth step. This is the opinions' level. They rise as a result of comparison between our interpretation (third step) and our expectations about what should happen. Here, our values and our preferences come into play. We decide on this step whether the situation is "fair" or "unfair", "pleasant" or "unpleasant", an "opportunity" or a "threat".
Now, we are ready to disembark on our fifth and final step. It is the actions' step. Based on the entire previous logic process, backed by our "ascension" through our inference ladder, we conclude certain actions are the most adequate to take care of our interests, given the situation we find ourselves in.

**Where is the inference ladder leaning on?**

We have to notice the set of observable data, or Facts, compose the first step, but not the "ground" where the ladder is leaning on.
Its "support" is, precisely, what we have been calling Mental Models.
Our reasoning logic and decision making process, with the following action execution, has its origin on that "set of beliefs and assumptions deeply ingrained, never questioned, DETERMINING HOW WE SEE THE WORLD AND HOW WE TAKE ACTIONS IN IT."
Or, in fewer words, the Inference Ladder is leaning on just one place: where OUR QUESTIONING STOPS.

The entire logic structure our action taking leans on is backed on what we believe in, what we suppose, what we take for granted. That is, precisely, what composes our mental models.

Everything we do, desire, want or reject, what we love or hate, has its origin on those mental models.
As an example, lets take a look at the following story.
We all know the story of "Little Red Riding Hood". Our parents, our grandparents, or our uncles or aunts have told us the story of the sweet little girl that meets an evil, wild wolf on her way to take food to her grandma.
We are used to listening the story from Little Red Riding Hood's point of view. Before our eyes (and ears) the situation looks like our mental model about little girls and wolves allows. However, there are other possible interpretations. Once, I heard a different version that told something like this:
*"The forest was my home. In it, I lived and cared much about how it looked. I tried to always keep it clean and neat. I really like the wild flowers and the new blossoms from the trees.*
*One sunny day, I was picking up the trash some inattentive tourists had left lying on the ground, when I heard some steps. As it there could have been danger, I ran to hide behind a tree. It was then when I saw the little girl walking down the path. She carried a basket on one of her arms and she was picking flowers on her way. I can't attest why, may be because of that attitude of picking new blossoms, or perhaps because she was dressed in a very strange way (all in red, and her head under a hood, as if she didn't want anyone to notice her), but I did not trust that little girl. Naturally, I stopped and asked her who she was, where she was coming from and where was she taking all of that. She answered by telling a strange story about her grandma, the long way and the short way and the basket with the lunch she was taking her.*
*She seemed honest, but she was in my dear forest, picking my flowers, and she certainly looked suspicious under her dress. So, I decided I should show her it wasn't right to be walking around the woods, hiding her face, and picking flowers. Obviously, I let her carry on, but I ran, getting ahead of her, until I reached her grandma's house. When I saw that nice old lady, I told her what I had thought, and she agreed her granddaughter needed to learn a lesson. We agreed she would not show herself until I called her, so she hid under the bed.*
*When the girl arrived and opened the door, I asked her to walk into the room, where I had laid, dressed as her grandma. The*

136

*girl came in, and when she saw me, she told me something disgusting about my "enormous ears". I had been insulted before so I tried to smooth things up, suggesting my "enormous ears" would help me listen better. I was trying to make her understand I liked her, so I wanted to pay close attention to what she said. But, she made another aggressive comment about my "bulging eyes". You can imagine how I was starting to feel in respect to this girl, that hid an aggressive and mean personality under her pretty looks. Still, I tried to overcome my anger telling her my bulging eyes helped me see her better. Her next insult really got me. It turns out I have a complex with my teeth, and she laughed about them by telling me how big they were. Now I know I should have controlled myself, but I didn't. I jumped out of bed and howled my teeth were big to "eat her better".*

*Lets be realistic: no wolf would ever eat a little girl. Everyone knows that. But, this crazy creature started running all around the house, yelling, while I followed her trying to calm her down. In order to show myself, I had taken off her grandma's clothes, but this made things even worse.*

*Suddenly, someone took down the door and the forest ranger showed up with his axe. I looked at him and it was very clear I was in trouble. There was a window behind me, so I made my escape quickly through it.*

*I would like to say that is the end of the story. But the grandma never told what had really happened. Word on the street was I was mean and despicable. Everyone began avoiding me...*

*I don't know what happened to that little girl in red, but if you care to know something about me: I have never lived happy and quiet since then."*

Perhaps, we are now in conditions to go back to our "logic chain" and make some modifications:
1-My beliefs are just that: beliefs. They are not the truth, but the result of my own inference process.
2-The final truth is not "obvious" for anyone, no matter how intelligent or well intended they are.
3-This "truth", even though is based on data about reality, does not include all data or information out there.

4-The data I selected only describe my experience, NOT reality.

That is why it is so important, when starting a conversation, that people are willing to expose their own perspective, always remembering their experience is conditioned by their own mental models, and that they are also willing to explore and inquire other people's perspective, acknowledging their experience always has a reasonable logic.
In every conversation, any interlocutor "ascends" their own inference ladder, making different interpretations and reaching to totally different action suggestions.
If the interlocutors need to coordinate actions, falling into the "trap of double forgetting", ergo, taking their mental models as the only true and reasonable description of reality, it is unlikely they will be able to get a positive result.

Of course, the key to avoiding these bad results it is not in stopping to make inferences, or trying to suppress our mental models. We have seen the latter is totally ineffective. And the former is absolutely impossible. Human beings cannot avoid inferring. The key opening the door to understanding lies in transforming the set of inferences laying within the indisputable mental models to explicit, conscious, and disputable stories.
Success, I must warn, is never guaranteed. However, if the willingness to take these steps, and the ability to proceed are matched, the probability of mutual understanding grows exponentially.
In order to do this, these are some suggestions:

- Acknowledging the data we observe are influenced by our personal interests.
- Making those interests explicit, communicating them in a clear, honest way.
- Realizing other interlocutors may have different observations (also true) complimenting our own.
- Remembering, based on those observations, each person will have different interpretations and conclusions as well. Acknowledging this process as absolutely

legitimate and sharing interpretations and opinions in a sincere way.
- Inquiring what data the interlocutors highlight.
- Exploring their logic chains and finding out their objectives.
- Asking for (and offering) examples and explanations, to make abstractions concrete.
- Explaining data, reasoning, and personal objectives. (This way we will be "descending" on our inference ladder at everyone's sight)
- At all times remembering there is nothing in our central nervous system allowing us to access other people's thoughts. If I want to know the inferences other people are making, I need to ask.

Our mental models are invisible. That is a great danger. But, treating the concept with honesty and care, it becomes an excellent tool for understanding the thinking structures. Own and other people's.
To achieve true communication with others, it will be crucial to work in a context of mutual respect, humbleness and comprehension.
This is a great challenge, given it implies transcending a mental model deeply ingrained in our society, governing most thinking processes: the know-it-all's mental model, which we have already talked about in previous chapters.

# Chapter 5
## The voice of consciousness

### Values, virtues and abilities

"The Russian Messenger" was one of Europe's most prestigious literary magazines on the XIX Century, a time particularly fertile for world literacy. First published in Moscow, and later in Saint Petersburg, their pages reflected a good portion of the "Golden Age" production of Russian literature. Between 1868 and 1869, its pages delivered one of the most brilliant works of Fedor Dostoyevski: "The Idiot".
The novel tells the story of Prince Lev Nikoláyevich Mishkin, a Russian nobleman, orphan since his sweet childhood. Prince Mishkin suffers of epilepsy and has been educated in an orphanage in Switzerland, where he spent his entire childhood and part of his youth. His sickness, added to his orphan condition and his peculiar education made of him a naive human being, saying what he thinks, not hiding his feelings and being extremely trustful. Mishkin believes everyone is nice, so he interacts that way with them.
These unusual characteristics for the Russian society during mid-nineteenth Century (as unusual as almost every society in the XXI Century), give him the nickname "idiot".
The Prince's sincerity and good faith are seen as a lack of maturity, as a defect, and far from being seen as a virtue, is a reason for mocking and lack of respect.
Mishkin's life is not an easy one and ends in a sad way. Throughout his life, he never reaches joy and happiness.

As it happens with every great piece of work of human genius, Prince Mishkin's story calls for deep reflection.
Why does someone with high moral values not reach immediate recognition from his congeners? What is it preventing him from getting his own happiness objectives?
I truly believe "The Idiot" is an excellent starting point to venture in a reflection about values, virtues and abilities.
The novel shows us it is not enough to have high values, if they do not move on to the more practical category of virtues, ergo, they do not completely turn into concrete abilities.

A value is a moral election. It means to take position about good and bad, right and wrong, beautiful and abject. A value is an absolute for the person adopting it, a master opinion that remains in time, acting as a permanent guide for that person's actions. Other than strange exceptions, which might be provoked by a major break in the person's life, values do not change. (There is a famous exception, which is a joke Groucho Marx made when asked about his values/principles: "Those are my principles, and if you don't like them... well, I have others!")
Virtue is the set of actions that are reflected IN PRACTICAL LIFE, what values declare. It is about actions, behaviors, not ideas, anymore.
A virtue is a recurrent behavior, inspired by a value the person has adopted.
Finally, ability is the competence to reach effectiveness in those behaviors. Ability allows virtue to take place. Without ability, virtue does not happen, or happens inefficiently. Aimed results are not reached.
In Prince Mishkin's story, he had values, but, many times, his abilities (or lack of them) would not let him generate the efficient behaviors that would give him the results he sought.

The same thing can happen to any of us. We can also be victims of our own lack of expertise to generate behaviors that comply with the double objective of honoring our values and reaching desired results.
This chapter focuses on one of the most complicated values to honor: Sincerity.
On this case, sincerity is the value, the moral absolute that guides our actions. The virtue will be "to tell the truth", which means ALWAYS adjusting our actions to the behaviors demanded by the value. Finally, the ability will be composed by the capacity to "say what we are thinking, without hiding anything and inciting grievances or damages."

We have said sincerity is a value that presents quite a complexity to disembark in effective action. Many times I have been questioned it is possible or, even, convenient to

respect this value. But, if sincerity is a value, can we apply it only sometimes? If we declare sincerity a value in our lives, can we adjust its use to our convenience?
I believe if we did this, we would be getting dangerously close to Groucho Marx' statement about values.

Perhaps, defining "sincerity" is a good first step to move forward and understand what we mean by it.
We can say a good definition is: "Making sure our public speech (what I am saying) is always identical to our private speech (what I am thinking)."
You must notice we say "identical" and not "similar". Sincerity demands that what we say is exactly the same to what we think. Anything else might be effective, or convenient to reach our objectives, but it will not be sincere.

Clearly, it is a big challenge. And, precisely, the size of this challenge explains that many times, since we do not have the abilities to adjust to the virtue of generating actions coherent with the value (on this case, the ability to say what I think without hurting anyone and without hiding anything), we think it is not always possible or convenient "being sincere".

In conclusion, the following reflections focus on three matters:
1-Value: Sincerity
2-Virtue: Accomplishing to say exactly what I am thinking
3-Ability: The art of telling the truth

**The Art of Telling the Truth**

Through a perspired window, the city was a choreograph of confusing figures, frantically dancing. The man looked once again at the bar's door, just as a reflex action. It had been a while he was not waiting to see anyone come in. Or better said, he did not believe anymore that anyone who would come in would make any difference to him. People were all brutally the same. It was late. Late in the day, and late in time.

He went back to his newspaper, and read for a fifth, or may be a ninth time, the old, morning headings. They did not mean much to him either. The coffee, cut with milk, had stopped steaming. He would not drink it anymore.

- Excuse me, may I sit?

The voice came over his head tilted at the newspaper. When he raised his eyes, he found its owner.

It was a woman about sixty years old. Her clothes, simple and quite clean, revealed that dignity and good taste are not lost with time. Her eyes lied a youth her skin would not show.

- May I sit? – She respectfully insisted. – I have walked too much. And the street, today, is not a good place to stay.

Never before in his life had he done something like it, but there was something about that woman he immediately liked. He asked her to sit, and treated her with something warm.

- Coffee and milk will be fine. It is the best thing to kill the cold and cheat the stomach.

While they waited for the waiter to bring the order, silence took over. Far from creating tension, it was a healing silence.

- You've got sad eyes, young man. – She said after a few minutes. – Would you care telling me what is going on? The advantage in talking with me is I don't know you, and probably you won't see me ever again. Fewer times you'll be safer, if telling the truth is what you need.

The man was left astonished. There, before him, was a woman he had never met before, she was offering a sort of silence confession he had not asked for, and better yet, her intromission turned to be seductively charming.

- It's been such a long time since I've spoken with anyone. Speaking the truth, I mean.
- Then, perhaps, you don't mind wasting some time talking with me.

It might have been he had done some gesture, or may have happened the silence that followed was interpreted as an acceptance, but the truth is the next thing the man heard was the start of a conversation that, he now knows, would change many things in his life...

Why is talking difficult for us?

Think for a moment. If you could choose, which of the characters would you like to be? What role do you think you would feel more comfortable in? For which of the two do you think you would have greater competence to perform? Would you talk, and say everything you think, without hiding anything? Or would you listen carefully, without making any judgments? Or, perhaps, is it possible you find out you are not capable of taking either role, given you current abilities?

On this piece of work I propose to explore the difficulties and incompetence preventing a productive communication, and generating breaks and mutual resentment in most cases.
We will check some language distinctions, which, used with humbleness, comprehension and respect, promise better results when embarking on decisive conversations in which there are subtle and complex matters in stake, which have an impact on our possibilities and those around us'.

Generally, the first difficulty in productively conversing rises from the basic attitude the interlocutors take. Both in professional and private life, when we converse we dedicate much less time to ask questions than explaining our point of view. We try to impose our own point of view, without exploring other people's perspectives. We even assume those that do not share our point of view have a secret motive, or are guided by some hidden intention. As a consequence, we begin to worry about "guessing" those motives and intentions but, obviously, do not declare we are doing it. This way, we generate ourselves a "hidden agenda" that ends up transforming what we say in the conversation into an incomplete similarity instead of what we are actually thinking. On one side and the other.

The first great mistake we make is assuming we have access to knowing other people's "intentions". We observe a behavior, a set of actions that someone else carries, and immediately assign an intention to it. However, we forget there is nothing in our nervous system (nor in the rest of our biology) letting us know other people's thoughts.

All we can see are actions, behaviors. Based on those actions we observe, we articulate a story, an explanation about the reasons of that behavior, but, while actions belong to other people, interpretations belong to ourselves.

Ken Wilber refers to this impossibility of having a direct access to what is on other people's minds on the following passage in "A Brief History of Everything":

"A brain expert, a neurophysiologist () can get to knowing everything about my brain but, ignore everything about the concrete contents of my mind because, to know the contents, he will need to talk with me. () It is about something truly extraordinary because, in case someone wanted to know what is going on in my mind, they would only have one way to know it: asking me. There is absolutely no other way that someone may know what are my thoughts unless they ask, talk and communicate with me. And if I don't want to tell them, they will never know the concrete content of my thoughts. Evidently, they can torture and force me to tell them but, in order to do that, they will have to talk. () In other words, (anyone wanting to know what is on my mind) will have to submit to a Dialogue –not a monologue –, will have to commit to an intersubjective exchange and stop studying me as an empirical investigation object, as an object of his empirical look."

Having this subtle matter present is crucial for starting a delicate conversation.

In second place, we focus in the "unproductive convincing". We deliver our own points of view as finished products, without ever exposing our thinking process. This way, our interlocutors cannot know the data we have worked with to get to such conclusions, nor the logic we have used, or the concerns we took care of.

Without any access to this information, it is impossible for them to find out more or offering other alternatives. They, at the same time, try to unproductively convince us of the kindness of their positions.

When we fall into the unproductive convincing, the conversation almost inevitably drifts onto a terrain of null inquiring, or, even worse, "disguised inquiring".
We make few, or none, questions. Or, we formulate rhetorical or ironic questions. The motive guiding those questions is not learning from the other, but to show how wrong the other is. And, of course, we are right.
Then, a phenomenon that Professor Fernando Bartolomeo taught me once, takes place: when two adults participating in a conversation have different points of view, they are much more oriented to fight than to learn.
It is like we felt more comfortable in the role of the know-it-all, who seeks to show he is right no matter what, even at the price of starting a complex fight. As if we were more trained to fight than opening our mind to new possibilities.

Every conversation has an objective. Or multiple ones. The problem is while some of them are expressed during it, others remain hidden.
These objectives, explicit as much as hidden ones, respond to our mental models. The mental model that prevails in the most committed conversations is the one of unilateral control.

This way, guided by the desire of controlling the situation, we start a process that ends up destroying every possibility for a mature dialogue.
One of the most imperious demands of the unilateral control mental model is "looking good". Never facing the chance of being hurt. Even though this might imply hiding what we think. As a complement, we reason that an excellent way to avoid injuries is avoiding the other getting hurt. This feeling, which at a first sight seems noble, becomes pernicious when it is the only thing guiding our actions during the conversation.
The result is we end up hiding what we really think, and we are fully convinced our interlocutor is doing the same thing.

What is it preventing us from saying what we really think? Which would be the consequences of saying exactly what we think? Which would be the consequences of not saying it? There is an interesting metaphor to explain what happens with what we really think, but never say.
Think about raw oil. It is a dark, viscous, smelly liquid. It is of no, or very little, use as long as it is not distilled. If you take some of that raw oil and throw it at someone else, how do you think that person will react? Most likely, this will start off a conflict. Evidently, we cannot do that if we want to have productive relations with other people.
Another possible option seems to be to keep the raw oil in our hands. Or, even worse, to "swallow" that burden. But, we all know we would get intoxicated. We cannot do that either if we want to have a long, prosper life.

Something similar happens with what we think but never say. If we do not say exactly what we think, it is because we suppose that, in case of saying spitting it out that way, we would create a conflict. There would be similar results as throwing raw oil at our interlocutor: fight, conflict and reprisal engage. Then, we choose not to say it. We "swallow" what we think. But this provokes anguish, frustration and anger.

If we say what we think, there are painful consequences. If we do not, it is the same deal. We desperately need to invent a third alternative.

The third alternative is processing our thoughts. Just like raw oil, which carefully distilled becomes an excellent energy source, what we think, even the most negative and painful thing, carefully processed and communicated, can become a really transforming possibility for mutual learning.

Working on a conversation

Remember a conversation that you might have had not long ago. Clearly, the conversation I am asking you to remember is not a random one. Firstly, the result of that conversation must have been frustrating for you. It is about one of those conversations in which we lose our track, we get away from the objectives we had in mind when starting it, we feel the conversation "becomes alive" and travels on lanes we would have never imagined or suspected.
Secondly, the conversation must have been important to you, and its consequences must not have been trivial. This second condition is crucial for the speculation we will make together. Given the conversation I ask you to remember is composes by the "raw materials" we will use to work with, it is important you consider it relevant, so the learning we get from this becomes relevant too. Finally, there is an additional condition that, despite it not being imperative, contributes a lot to the process: it is preferred the chosen conversation be, besides complying with the two previous requirements, recurrent. Every time you engage on it, the frustrating results should appear.
Once you have "found" the required conversation, I ask you try remembering the most important part of it. Try to "re-listen" what was said. What you said as much as the words your interlocutor said. Here, you are committed to adjust as best as you can to the conversation that took place. As if you "un-taped" what you said. Take a piece of paper and, after drawing a vertical line to create two columns, re-write the conversation on the right one.

Now, lets do a little experiment. Try remembering everything you were thinking, but never said during the conversation. Focus on it. What were your feelings, thoughts about the situation and interlocutor? What was your state of mind? How did this change as the conversation developed?

Write all of this on the left column. Now, look at the results:
As you will probably notice, when you talk with someone else, you have two simultaneous conversations: your public

conversation (what you say) and your private conversation (what you think).
What happens in the type of conversations we are exploring is that a gap forms between one and the other. At all times, you shut up more than you speak up. Or shut the most important thing. The raw oil becomes to accumulate.

Lets speculate about the potential consequences of saying what you thought but did not say, if you said it exactly like you were thinking. You probably would have started a fight, a break, a conflict. You would have hurt and been hurt.

Luckily, you did not do that. It is not about saying it that way. It is not about throwing raw oil at your interlocutor. This is a more subtle matter.
Lets reflect for a moment about the consequences of not having said what was thought. Here, we do not need to speculate. You only have to remember what happened. Feelings like anguish, frustration, impotence and anger arise. This is the raw oil circulating through our digestive system. We cannot keep this situation for a long time. The consequences are disastrous if we do it. And, if at some point, tired of "swallowing toxic waste", we let everything we think out, without processing it, we will inflict all the harm we attempt to avoid when shutting up.

What should we do, then? The alternative is processing our "bad" thoughts. Distilling what we have thought but did not say. Taking the explosive charge off. And, simultaneously, keeping its meaning. The process we will explore has as objective saying what we think, what is true to us, without hurting others or betraying ourselves. It is about taking the raw oil and transforming it into an energy resource.

A small digression between true and the truth

Before we begin to reflect about what I like calling the Art of Telling the Truth, I believe it is important to remember some ideas and intuitions we have already referenced on previous chapters. It is about the matter of human perception.

Human beings have a mental map of the reality around us. Every time we take a look at the world, on every occasion we get close to it, all we can do is perceiving a portion, a part, of an immeasurable reality for our eyes. Our mental models are always biased. They are a set of assumptions and beliefs deeply ingrained in us. They do not only determine what we see in the world, its shape, but also how we design it and take actions in it.

Therefore, when we try telling the truth, we need to have always present that despite our efforts for perfectly adjusting to it, the best we will accomplish will be humbly expressing the part of the truth that, to our eyes, appears evident. When attempting to say the truth, all we will accomplish will be saying what is true to us. Our commitment will be with precision, sincerity and respect. It will never be with the true "truth".

A crucial distinction: Observations and Opinions

To continue with our experiment, lets introduce one of the Ontology of Language's most powerful distinctions: Observations versus Opinions.

If you observe the piece of paper on which this work is written, you will notice you can distinguish in it a set of characteristics. You will be able to say, for example, the paper is white. You will also be able to say it is neat. Those two statements seem to be referring to the paper. If we represent them in a simple way, we can say both phrases respond to the same structure, the common structure for statements:

I state X equals Y.

On these statements, Y is characterizing X. There are, however, crucial differences between the sentences "The paper (X) is white (Y)" and "The paper (X) is neat (Y)". Even though they both are statements, the former is an example of what we will call observations, while the latter is an example of an opinion or judgment.

As we said, they are both statements, since what they are doing is stating that X presents (or has) certain characteristics. What makes them different, and from my point of view, crucially different, is the commitment the observer takes when saying one or the other.

**Observations**

In the case of observations, the commitment taken by the observer is providing evidence of what he has said. Observations take the general form:

X is Y

When I say the paper is white, I am talking about a characteristic that belongs to the paper. It is about a state of mind that is not modified by my way of referring to it. What we could call (according to Rafael Echeverría) adjustment direction between the world and the word, takes a road in which the world leads and the word follows. If I want my observation to seem happy, I ought to adjust my saying with great precision, looking to describe a state of mind that is previous (and independent, at least until a certain point) to my observation. The characteristic of being white is something that belongs to the paper. Within a community sharing a biological structure and a set of linguistic distinctions, I will be able to provide evidence of my sayings, if someone should dispute the characteristic that I have given to the paper.

The commitment of providing evidence happens to be greatly important for constructing our own identity. If, every time we talk, one way or another, we are committing before the community listening to us, when we make an observation, we put quite an important part of our public identity in stake.
Observations, given their peculiar nature, can be either true or false. When an observer makes an observation, he commits to the truth of his statements. Whoever might be listening to him should draw conclusions of what they have heard, contrasting the observation with the state of the world they perceive. In the case the observation is disputed, it is highly important for

the observer to be in conditions of holding what he has said, providing evidence. If he cannot do it, it will be concluded his observation was false. And his public identity will be injured. People who recurrently make false observations are called either ignorant or liars. While the ignorant (or mistaken) makes a false observation believing it is true, the liar makes a false observation being aware of its fallacy, attempting to deceive or mislead.

Due to either motive, it is really difficult coordinating actions with people that make false observations.

Although it seems simple to determine whether an observation is true or false, it is important to analyze the process by which the bases are established for the members of a linguistic community to make observations.

Firstly, we have an observation's existence condition. It is what I will call declaration context. Every observation always exists within a context that gives meaning to it.

This piece of significance is determined by declarations pre-existent to the observation, which let it make sense, to mean something for the members of the community.

In our example of "the paper is white", any observer belonging to the biolinguistics community, for which "white" has a clear meaning, will be able to prove whether the observation is true or false. And he will be able to do it because he shares a context in which the declaration of what is white is previous to the observation.

A declaration is a language act through which a declarant with authority to do so stipulates an identity. The declaration takes the shape of:

**I declare X is X.**

A declaration creates worlds. If we accept language is generative, we will understand a declaration is the generative linguistic act by excellence.

When we make a declaration, we are taking the commitment of validating its authority, in the case it is questioned. There are multiple sources for that authority, given it can be backed by wisdom, moral, personal history, or even strength. Many

declarations that generated realities in the history of mankind were made backed by the authority strength gives. In my opinion, too many times.
Whichever the origin of the authority, declarations compose the language of power.

Each community shares a set of declarations accepted as valid, allowing making observations within that community. Doctors, lawyers, or accountants, for example, make their observations based on the declaration context they share. When the declaration context we move in changes, we change the set of true observations we can make. The realities that we can describe with our true observations change along with the declaration context.
When two people try to communicate, they must make sure they share a declaration context. Otherwise, it will be very complex to understand each other.

Secondly, there is an observation relevance context. When we say, "the paper is white", we are focusing our attention in a partial aspect of the reality around us. Think briefly about the extraordinary amount of things you could say, for example, about what is happening while you read this book. You could make reference to the writing per se, its content, the font type it is written in, the language, the line spacing, the literary style, the phrases extension, etc. Also, you could focus your attention on the room you find yourself in, or the house or apartment, the building, the neighborhood, the city, the country, the continent, etc. You could make observations about any of those aspects. We could go crazy if we were not capable of focusing our attention on a specific and partial aspect of the reality. When saying, "the paper is white", we choose to distinguish an aspect that is relevant for us from an immeasurable reality.
This choice is determined by the observation relevance context. Such context responds to the interests and worries we have each time we choose to distinguish an object or phenomenon, to make an observation about it.

The selection process has its origin in our traditions, history, tastes, our community's history, experiences, our way of operating and our objectives.

Every time two people try communicating, they have to build bridges between their respective relevance contexts. This way, they will achieve what is in stake to be important for both of them, while they will be able to understand the reasons motivating them to focus their attention on different aspects of the reality.

Finally, when making an observation, if besides from making it true, you want the observer wants it to be effective, he needs to keep in mind the application background. It is not enough for the observation to be precise. If, during a business conversation, a partner asks another one, "How many vehicles do we have in our disposition?" the answer will have to do with the cars and trucks the firm disposes of, but surely it will not include their particular vehicles, nor their respective wives' or family's.

All effective observation is applicable to a background. Therefore, when trying to communicate, it is important that the people involved share such background. Otherwise, their observations, though precise and honest, will be ineffective.

Seen with these distinctions, when a disagreement regarding an observation is produced, an unbeatable learning opportunity is presented. We will be before the opportunity of exploring different mental models, different ways to experience the world, various declaration contexts, different interests and worries, and diverse application backgrounds. Two human beings seeking to communicate effectively will have to keep in mind each of these possible-coupling levels.

**Opinions**

While an observation can be true or false, opinion will never be one or the other. The commitment an observer takes when emitting an opinion is not with the precision of his words, but with utility and validity.

Even though opinions are completely different from observations regarding the commitment taken by the declarer, their appearance is quite similar. Their essence is different, but their aspect might confuse us. Opinions also take the shape:

**X is Y.**

This similarity is, no doubt about it, the source of a great portion of the anguish, mismatches, low productivity and stress we face when we try to communicate with other human beings.

With opinions, language puts us in a trap. At first sight, it seems, when emitting an opinion, saying X is Y, we are (just like with observations) describing X having Y characteristics. Here, however, rises a great difference: While observations talk about the object, individual or phenomenon observed, opinions talk about the observer.

When we emit an opinion, far from describing something "external" to us, we are referring to a personal experience. The opinion describes the observer; it gives away his standards, preferences, paradigms and personal and social history. An opinion always means taking position, an evaluation, through which the observer reveals his perspective before an experience that takes as personal.

Human beings have opinions permanently. As we can see on the exercise we did involving the conversation I asked you to remember, we sometimes express publicly our opinions, and sometimes we do not.

We can control what we say, but we do not control what we think. It is not about learning not to have opinions, but about learning to know what to do with them.
We cannot choose the opinions we have, or the moment at which we have them. Judgments just simply occur. As human beings, we are destined to have opinions, constantly. Most likely, right now, you are having an opinion on the quality of this work, or about my competence to explain a topic.

However, you had not programmed this. At the moment you started to read this, you had not planned to have an opinion on what you were about to read. Judgment simply appears. The same happens on our daily life.

Of course there is nothing wrong in emitting judgment. Friedrich Nietzstche used to say human beings are "animals that can judge". I believe, this way, he reminded us that, since we cannot escape the imperative of giving sense to our lives, we are "damned" to giving value to our actions. The action of giving value to our actions is done through opinions. Judgments are the engine of our actions. This is one of the most important aspects of the theory of human action that motivates this work. Just as I see it, and my professors have showed me, there is a complex phenomenon surrounding opinions:
1. We have opinions all the time
2. We cannot choose the opinions we have
3. We operate on the basis of our opinions

Seen this way, we understand how important it is for human beings to know what to do with their opinions. If we operate on the basis of opinions we cannot chose, then, how do we make our lives develop the way we want them to? The answer I am trying to articulate explains us even though we cannot choose our opinions, we can choose what to do with them.

Opinions are amazingly powerful. They have an explosive potential capable of generating new worlds; they open and shut possibilities. If we check the most important events in our lives, we will see behind each choice, behind every path walked, there is an evaluation we have realized, which composed the pillar we lean on to aim towards a certain direction, discarding all the other possible alternatives.
And, given we act according to the opinions that different alternatives and experiences require, we are obliged to acknowledging the decisive role our opinions play in the generation of our identity. Like Rafael Echeverría states, "judgments determine people's identity core."

We have said the most important generative language act is declaring. Opinions are a special case of declaration. To give opinions value, opposed to declaration that only need to be backed by the authority they are emitted with, they need of a careful argumentation process.

Before exploring this process, I believe it is adequate to remember opinions can be either valid or invalid. It does not matter what we do, how rigorously we undergo the process of grounding an opinion, it will never become an observation, it will never be either true or false.

Every time we emit an opinion, we do it for something. There is always an interest we take care of when passing judgment. This connects the opinion with the future, given that when we emit it, we take care of something we worry about and aim when judging. Depending on the opinion we formulate, certain actions might seem possible, while others will be discarded.
The interest they take care of is a crucial dimension in the process of grounding opinions.
Further, in order to be founded, opinions need to be backed by observations. For example, when we say "Lucy is an excellent lawyer", we do it because we have seen her working, we have seen how much time she takes to prepare a case and check backgrounds, how many times her clients have won judgments, etc. If someone asked us why were she a good lawyer, it would not be valid to say that she seems rigorous and enterprising. This way, we would be grounding an opinion (good lawyer) with two other opinions (rigorous and enterprising). Judgments that pretend to be grounded need to be backed by observations about behaviors; ergo, precise descriptions about actions that have happened. The more recurrent the action (the greater the amount of true, available data), better grounded the opinion will be.

A third opinion dimension is composed by standards. When emitting judgment, we assume a set of behavior expectations before which we ought to take the actions supporting the opinion. Generally, many of the opinion in which we base our actions respond to social standards, to generally accepted behaviors, which, many times, we do not check. It is convenient paying close attention to this phenomenon, given it is not strange we discover we have been acting according the "socially" accepted opinions, rather than our own ones. There is a huge difference between operating on the basis of our own opinions and operating on the basis of opinions we believe are ours.

Even though most standards we use to validate our opinions are generally accepted by the community, sometimes there are individuals whose actions are recurrently over such standards. We are talking about transformative leaders and innovators. In our chapter about learning, we have called these individuals Masters.

Clearly, every time we have an opinion it will not always be about a behavior. We also have opinions about phenomena or objects. On this case, we evaluate their appearance. For example, we can say, "there is a lot of snow at the base of Cerro Catedral." Here, we are not giving an opinion about actions pertaining to the mountain, but about the aspect it presents at a certain moment. The standards we use on these cases come from customs and personal and social traditions.

Standards take us to a fourth opinion dimension: their application domain. A domain is a space of permanent interests, in which we identify the possibility of certain, recurrent breaks. Every standard refers to a domain. If what we are doing is evaluating behaviors, the domain involved will be a domain of action. Otherwise, if we are giving an opinion about appearances, then the domain will be a domain of observation.

If I say, 'Stephen is a good driver", my opinion will not mean the same if I am making reference to the domain of driving a streetcar than to the domain of a Formula One car. On the different opinion application domains, the reference standards change. Behaviors that can be accepted, or even very well seen, respecting a certain domain, can be unacceptable in a different one.

An opinion can be well grounded, which means it has been through the process of checking the four previous dimensions, and still not be valid. Therefore, the fifth opinion dimension is the authority that it is emitted with.
Anyone can make a judgment, but not anyone can emit a valid judgment. To have value, the person giving the opinion must have the authority to do so. Contrarily, the opinion could be well grounded, but it will still be invalid, useless in terms of the reality it can generate. For example, lets look at the case of a fan watching a **fútbol** match. This person can evaluate the players' behavior and draw the conclusion that one of them is not taking actions that justify his presence on the field. He can even ground his opinion very well, making reference to the generally accepted standards, to that player's recurrent actions during the current and past games, he can perfectly restrict his opinion application domain and have a legitimate interest (he can be a loyal fan of the team that player plays for). But, he is not the team's head coach. His opinion lacks authority to generate a new reality (which, on this case, would mean a substitution for another player). There is nothing wrong in the fan having an opinion about the players. What it is wrong is to pretend this opinion to generate a change on the match's score. Only the coach of the team, based on his own opinions about his players' competence, has the authority to make changes on the line up.

This connection between opinions and authority should not seem strange, since we have said the opinion is a special case of declaration. And, we have seen that the crucial element of a declaration is, precisely, the authority of the person emitting it. Thus, the following, simple, "equation":

GROUNDED OPINION + AUTHORITY = VALID OPINION

It is important to see this authority matter connects judgments with the language power.
We say there is power when there is capacity to generate effective actions, within a certain domain. Then, the authority to realize judgments is one of the greatest sources of power people in general, and managers particularly, can count with.

Within a firm, the people that, for any given reason, have the authority to emit opinions have the key for productivity, efficiency and organizational and personal development.

**The Sincerity matter regarding opinions**

Now, we fall into the matter of sincerity when emitting opinions.
In more than an opportunity, my students have asked me if, despite everything we have explained, I believed opinions could actually be true. The explanation that supports such questioning is presented as follows:

- "An opinion can be true or false"—says the student —"given that when I say that Alice is a good person, I am convinced she is. Therefore, I am not lying; I am saying the truth of what I think. This way, the opinion that Alice is a good person becomes a true opinion."

On this case, I believe the problem is the confusion underlying in not distinguishing the opinion from the description of the opinion.
On one hand, we have the opinion "Alice is a good person". This phrase is part of the individual's private conversation, what he thinks. Then, the person can express publicly his thought. In order to do that, he can precisely describe what he thinks, so he will say "Alice is a good person". He will be emitting an opinion, and he will be doing it through a precise description of his opinion.
If we look carefully, we can draw the conclusion we actually have two phrases, and one of them will be the opinion:

"Alice is a good person."

The other will be the description of such opinion, which can be expressed the following way:

"The precise description of my judgment about Alice is that I think she is a good person."

This second phrase is a description (observation) of the opinion. Then, this observation can be either true or false. If the person expresses publicly his opinion about Alice, describing her precisely, such description will be true. If, he does not do it this way, his observation will be false.
But, the opinion (Alice is a good person) will continue to be grounded or ungrounded, never true or false.

I say this matter takes us to the dimension of sincerity within opinions given that we will say the public expression of an opinion is sincere when the observation describing such opinion is precise, ergo, true.

Sincerity, although it is an opinion dimension, in the end, it refers to the truth or fallacy of the observations about such opinions.
In our example, the phrase "The precise description of my judgment about Alice is that I think she is a good person", is the observation that, talking about Alice, can be analyzed on its sincerity, thus, its truth or fallacy value.

**Opinions and Temporality**

Every time we emit a judgment, we are not only exposing who we are, but also manifesting the temporal structure that dictates our lives. Human beings have a present, past and a future. As people, we live in a certain historic personal and social moment (the present), we are the result of a set of personal experiences and social events (the past), and we are moved by the completion of plans, projects and goals that have not happened yet, but impact on our lives anyways (the future). Opinions relate these three temporal instances.

Firstly, judgments are declarations referred to the characteristics of an individual, an object or phenomenon, claimed by an observer in the present. Thus, opinions refer to an observer's present experience.

Further, there is the past. When backing on recurrent observations about previous behaviors (in the case of a judgment about a behavior) or past events (in the case of opinions about objects, phenomena or processes), judgments refer to what happened.

Then, opinions refer to the past.

Finally, every time we give a valid opinion, we are taking care for a particular interest. This interest takes us to what has not happened yet, what we still do not have, manifesting the most important opinion temporal dimension: the future.

Valid judgments always project towards the future. Even more so, we make judgments because we are worried about our future. If we did not care about what is about to happen, it would not make any sense to emit opinions. They condense our past experiences, and lead them to the future. The future gives us a focal point from which we express our opinions. The relationship goes both ways: opinions are oriented towards the future, and it is the future we desire what motivates having an opinion, taking a position regarding the present.

This is a good time to attempt clarifying a matter I believe to be important. Given their temporal nature, opinions are open to change. There is nothing wrong in changing them, and in fact, with the exception of a few opinions about good and bad we sustain through a long period of time (sometimes a lifetime), which we call "Values", an intelligent individual who wants to learn, permanently checks his own opinions and, if he finds arguments to do it, changes them for others.

Changing an opinion is not a symptom of incoherence, but intelligence, if we do it based on solid arguments that improve previous ones making us having a different opinion. This happens all the time, and it is only natural, given our human nature. We even have, on many occasions, contradictory opinions before the same situation. As Woody Allen brilliantly said: "Thoughts I don't share come to my mind."

Human nature is, many times, contradictory. And, like Walt Whitman used to say: "Very well, then I contradict myself, I am large, I contain multitudes."

I repeat, there is nothing wrong in it. What it is important is the adoption of an opinion against others happens after a rigorous process of argumentation.

### How to "refine" our thoughts

Processing or "refining" an opinion implies a rigorous process of verification regarding the different judgment dimensions. It is about looking for tools to distinguish a valid (or useful) opinion from an invalid (or useless) one.

The first thing becoming evident when "distilling our opinions" is, once again, the crucial distinction there is between judgments and observations.

An observation's verification is easy to do. All we have to do is contrasting what we say with the data from the portion of the reality they attempt to describe. If they match, we will say it is true; if they do not, it will be false. However, what is an advantage when it comes to simplicity, it becomes a disadvantage in terms of power. Observations are very limited in regards to the opening of possibilities. They lack, among other things, the temporal structure opinions have. For example, when someone says there are 68 degrees Fahrenheit of temperature, without evaluating whether that condition favors or not the comfort inside a room, interrupts the context creativity to decide whether to use the room for te imminent board meeting.

Opinions are not as concrete and definitive as observations. They are always open to the possibility of being checked. They are more flexible and changing. They are also more powerful in terms of opening or shutting possibilities. Since they have a temporal structure, they can be modified in the future.

Because they are such a powerful distinction, opinions like Medusa`s poison, can cause goodness as well as harm. Many times, they are the source of pain and distressing breaks. This is why we need a process of rigorous verification of our judgments.

First of all, it is necessary to appropriate our opinions. Therefore, it is crucial remembering we are talking about judgments, which are declarations describing us. They are affirmations that instead of describing the person, object or process in question, they talk about the standards of the observer about the person, object or process he is describing.

The act of appropriating seeks to overcome a subtle trap language puts. When we emit an opinion, we do it under the general equation "X is Y". We say, for example, that "Nick is incompetent", and when we do this, we believe we are describing Nick. We assume the characteristic Y describes X; that it belongs to it. Since we have learnt the predicate talks about the subject, we perceive that given Nick is the subject in the phrase, incompetent is a characteristic that composes the predicate, so it talks about how the subject is. It tells us how Nick is.

We find ourselves before a trap, as I said before. And, just as I see it, it is a tragic trap. The lineal and unidirectional characteristic of our language does not let us see the opinions' natural essence. In judgments, the predicate never talks about the subject. It talks about the observer of that subject. Here, in opinions, emerges with all its might that phrase Humberto Maturana said: "everything said, is said by someone."

That someone (the observer, declarer, giving the opinion) manifests the opinion belongs to him, who he is, what are his interests, his standards and expectations, the action domain that is important for him and what actions he has chosen to mark as relevant.

However, the phrase "Nick is incompetent" hides all of this. When we listen to it, we think we know how Nick is. To get out of this trap, we need to build a different sentence. It is necessary we appropriate our opinions. That is, lets talk in a way manifesting without a doubt that the observer is the one in stake in the sentence. And if the phrase is ours, it will be us who emerge in the opinion.

Then, the search focuses on finding a declaration that, keeping the essence of what we wanted to explain with our opinion, manifests at the same time we are talking about ourselves. We need to build a phrase in which we appear as the subject.

If what we want to say is, "Nick is incompetent", we can express the same meaning by saying: "I think Nick is incompetent."
In this declaration, Nick is not the subject anymore. Now, the subject of this sentence is Me. It is a happier way to express I am talking about myself.
However, even though we have progressed in the appropriation process, it is not enough yet.
Still, the way Nick is appears at the core of the matter. We still talk about him.

A better way to express the essence of what we wanted to say could be: "I do not like certain actions Nick takes." Here, the subject still is Me, but I am not talking about Nick anymore. I am talking about his actions. And this opens a world of new possibilities. For Nick and myself.
On the first place, when attempting to characterize an individual the way we usually do (the way you did in the conversation in our exercise), we seem to say: "I declare the world is divided between competent and incompetent people (in our example). That has been, is, and will be. And I ask my listeners to agree with me that Nick is that way."
So much anguish, frustration, battling and low productivity held in this way of expressing ourselves! It has an explosive charge. Escalation and confrontation become inevitable.
There are no possibilities for either Nick or myself. We are damned to a situation that cannot change. Given he cannot change how he is, and I cannot change my affirmation.

When appropriating, everything changes. When we refer to actions, possibilities that remained shut suddenly open. It is possible that, metaphysically speaking, Nick cannot change who he is, his essence. But, all human beings have the chance of changing our actions.
When we deeply understand that it is not the person I dislike, or bothers or even threatens me, but his actions, I can understand there is a possibility of opening a conversation about such actions.
The process of appropriating gives room to a mutual learning conversation. Far from trying to impose our point of view, we

should explore the differences, trying to see what the other person can see but remains hidden for us. The conversation's spirit is learning, not trying to be right.
During this conversation, it will be greatly important to put in action the three fundamental values of learning: humility, compassion and respect.
As Thomas Merton, an American poet that became a Trappist monk, said in "Truth and Violence":
"The basic fallacy is composed by the lie that we are completely dedicated to the truth, and we can be dedicated to the truth in a way which is honest and exclusive at the same time: that we have the monopoly of the absolute truth, just like our occasional rival has the monopoly of the absolute error. Then, we convince ourselves we will not be able to preserve our vision purity, nor our inner sincerity if we begin a dialogue with the enemy, since he will corrupt us with his error. Finally, we believe truth cannot be preserved unless we destroy our enemy—because, given we have related him with the error, destroying his is destroying the error.

Of course, the rival has the same thoughts and basic policy for which he defends the "truth" about us.
He has related us with dishonesty, insincerity and fallacy. He thinks if we are destroyed, the truth will remain victorious.

If we actually pursued the truth, we would start by slowly taking away all our layers of fiction and deceit, one by one, or at least we should wish to do so, since merely desiring does not make us capable of doing it. Quite contrarily, our rival we want to destroy is the one that can point out our error and help us see it. The same way, we can help him notice his error, and that is the reason why he wants to destroy us.
But, in the long run, nobody can show the other the error inside him unless the other is convinced that his critic first sees and loves the good inside him. Therefore, while we desire to tell our rival he is wrong, we will never be able to do it effectively until we can notice what he is right on. And we will never appreciate his judgment about our errors until he shows he really appreciates our own, peculiar truth. Love, just love, for our own, peculiar truth. Love, just love, for our concrete

and mistaken other, in his deceit and sin: only this can open the door for truth.

As long as we do not have this love, as long as this love is not active or effective in our lives (given words and good intentions will never be enough), we will not have real access to the truth. At least, not to the moral truth."

Only in the spirit of humility and deep comprehension that take to unconditional respect (our definition of love), is how we will be able to really appropriate our opinions and build, alongside the other, the bridges that allow true understanding.

Of course, appropriating does not mean losing rigor, or leaving aside legitimate arguments holding our opinions. Conversely, it is the first step of a process during which we should expose those arguments with strictness and discipline. To be a comprehensive, humble and respectful person does not imply being week or fearful. The true strength is composed over the base of the legitimate doubt and the apprentice spirit.

Once we have appropriated our judgment, with not restrictions or deceits, we can move forward on its process. The second step we have to take consists of exploring the interest that led us to our opinion. Every time we have a valid opinion, it emerges responding to a matter we care about. All judgments aiming to be grounded need to comply with this condition of taking care of a certain interest. If I say, for example, that a truck with a front-wheel drive is better than a rear one, I would be referring it is better for something. Generally, we prefer cars with front-wheel drive when living in places that get snowed or where there are plenty of dirt roads. When saying this type of truck is better, we are taking responsibility of the particular interest that means driving inconveniently through snowy or muddy roads. Without considering the interest, if it does not exist or it is not clear, we will not have the opportunity of giving rigor to our opinions; they will not take care of any future possibility, hence, they will lose their value. Interest, which we take care of when giving an opinion, projects judgments towards the future. When we have an

opinion, and wish to ground it with rigor and discipline, we have to be capable of answering questions like these:
Can I clearly determine what am I taking care of when giving this opinion?
What is the worry my judgment aims towards?
What am I lacking, worrying about? What is making me happy or motivating me that makes me have this opinion?
What is the future I want to build? What possibilities is my judgment opening or shutting?
How are the future and the present connected through my opinion?
Of course, when (like in the case of our exercise) not only our opinions are in stake, but also other people's, it is very beneficial to explore together the answers one or the other would give to those questions.
This is precisely what we call productive inquiring.
Openly exploring, with humility, comprehension and mutual respect, the different interests that motivated the different opinions for each person.
Every process that I can carry out with my own opinions can be realized with my interlocutor's opinions. It is my responsibility to find ways to help him in this exploration.

When expressing and knowing the interests that move us, the possibilities of creating coexistence spaces grow. Mutual interests will be the bridges we ought to build with people around us to generate a way of being together based on acceptance.
Only once we have established these shared interests, only when we agree we all care about certain things in common, we will be in conditions of continuing with our opinion processing.

The third step consists of finding a solid base on which our opinions can be supported. We have already appropriated them, and we have detected the interest generating them. Now is time to give them a concrete body.
Every valid opinion needs to be backed on recurrent observations of the past. If we are dealing with opinions about behaviors, those observations will describe actions the

individual (or group of people) has taken. If what we evaluate is a phenomenon or process, we deal with observations about the occurrence of certain facts.

If, for example, I want to support the opinion that October is rainier than January in Mar del Plata, I will need to show a record of precipitations during both months on that area. But, if I want my opinion to be grounded, it will not be enough by showing the record of just one year. Instead, I will have to provide evidence of a set of years. The longer the range presented, the more grounded my opinion will be.

This distinction becomes essentially important in judgments about behaviors. When using our opinions with the objective of characterizing someone else, the danger doubles. On one hand, we have seen the first risk we face is "forgetting" it is about a judgment that does not describe someone else, but describes ourselves, declarers of the opinion. The second risk has its origin on the incapacity to "remember" that the temporal structure of judgments is based on actions. And actions are subject to change.

When we look at someone's behavior, all we can see are his actions. We do not have access to either his intentions, or his thoughts, or how he will be in the future. We only see his present actions or remember his past ones.

Of course we can suppose that if a person has behaved in a certain way in the past, he will do so similarly in the future. Precisely, this is one of the most powerful characteristics of opinions, allowing us to venture in the future with the presumption of particular certainties. However, we should not overlook that while past actions are factual and final events of a reality that has happened, the opinions we give regarding the future do not have the same certainty. They can be better or worse grounded, but will never be true or false.

Given the characteristics of actions, an observer will be able to say whether the action happened or not. Meaning we can attest, through observations, that it is either true or false the action took place. When we understand this peculiarity actions have, their observable nature, we get closer to two crucial matters: first, that valid opinions are backed on observations, not on other opinions.

Many times, when we try to give rigor or justification to our opinions, we fall in the error of backing a judgment on other judgments. It is very common, for example, to hear someone say, "Elizabeth is a good employee", and if someone asks the reason why she is a good employee, the answer is "because she is very neat, educated and very compliant".
As you have probably noticed already, neat, educated and compliant are also opinions about Elizabeth. This way of grounding opinions is the source of great confusions, disappointments and confrontations. However, it is very different to say, "I think Elizabeth is a really good employee because I have given her ten tasks this last week and she has completed all of them. When completing these tasks, I saw how she worked with other people and proved she hasn't confronted any of them. Further, during this last year, she hasn't been absent to work at all."
Completing ten tasks, not confronting people and not being absent are perceptible actions, they either happened or not, they can be described with observations. And it is very different to support our opinions on true observations than on the base of false observation or on unfounded judgments.

Second, what happened in the past, even though it is true it happened, can change in the future.
This is a greatly important matter. Fully comprehending it opens the door to an understanding of the human phenomenon that is filled with new possibilities. When we categorize someone (us, included), we are not describing a situation that cannot change. Quite contrarily, we are saying based on the evidence of a set of actions composing a past behavior, we draw the conclusion the person moves within a certain range of current possibilities.
That range of current possibilities determines the judgment we have about the individual, but if that range becomes wider, if the person changes the actions he is capable of doing and carries out new and different actions (which, as we have seen,

learning provides), the opinion we have about him will change as well.

If we go back to our example that "Nick is incompetent" and we analyze it from this point of view, we should notice that, even though we can observe a set of actions Nick has taken and we do not see adequate (actions defining Nick's range of current possibilities), it is also possible Nick changes his way of acting by learning new skills and abilities, and when carrying out these new actions, he will not seem incompetent for us anymore, but the opposite.

The fourth step in the process of refining our opinions consists of expressing and clarifying each interlocutor's expectations.
Having walked all the path up to this point, we have learnt to appropriate our judgments, inquired and expressed the interest motivating us, and we have agreed on which are the recurrent actions of the past that support them. Yet, it is still possible we keep the original opinion, simply because we find it well grounded. If, after checking all these steps, we find our opinion is moved by a legitimate interest and is backed on valid observations, we should reach to the correct conclusion it is a well-grounded opinion.

Nonetheless, this does not guarantee it is valid for our interlocutor. After talking with Nick, and having done the entire refining process thus far, it may happen he accepts our interest and agrees his action have been the ones we have highlighted, but still be satisfied and in peace with what he has done.

Then, this is the moment to ask for his authorization to open a conversation about new possibilities. This petition for his authorization to talk with him about a topic concerning us is vital. Without it, meaning Nick does not give us authority to make judgments about how convenient his actions have been, the opinions we have about him can be grounded, but will never be valid. An opinion is valid when the declarer has authority to give it. And this authority, at least in a transformative and learning conversation like this one, always comes from the person the opinion is about.

Only if our interlocutor gives us such authorization we will be able to move on. Contrarily, we have to accept the refusal and, since we consider our opinion well grounded, we should decide what are the steps to follow in the future. Even after traveling this path with hope, respect and rigor, it may happen we do not reach to an understanding. Life never promises results. And there are relationships that end. Being able to accept it implies wisdom and dignity.

However, there is always the chance we get the authority to move on. If we handled the situation with the artistry humility, comprehension and respect provide, this is the most likely scenario.

In that case, we should take care of the last step in the refining process: the conversation about expectations.

This is, from my point of view, the greatest transformative conversation. When opening the expectations conversation, we start to explore the world the way we would like it to be. It is not about explaining how the world should be, but merely expressing, with humility and respect, our desires, likes and dreams. It is about building bridges, looking for an agreement, constructing together a shared space. Asking the other to take certain actions, offering to take others ourselves. In the expectations conversation, the soul is the one speaking. And the soul's voice is incredibly transformative.

It is possible our interlocutor is not willing to comply with some of our wishes. Again, we have to unconditionally accept such decision and, in our legitimate right, design what actions to take. An alternative is abandoning the attempt, eventually, if we considerate it convenient, ending the relationship. Another option is to try new paths and explore new possibilities. Each one of us knows the point up to which we are willing to explore and check own and other people's expectations. The art of negotiating also has a lot to do with these conversational abilities.

Whether we reach to an agreement or not (and my experience tells me we get it most times), success is not guaranteed. Failure is not a possibility in a learning conversation as it is in an expectations conversation. Worst-case scenario, we would have painfully learnt that a relationship is no longer sustainable. Even then, this is better than deceit or self-deceit.

**Going back to our conversation**

Lets go back to our exercise. There, on that paper, you have a frustrating conversation. If you read this work this far, you now have distinctions you were not capable of doing earlier, you have acquired new conceptual tools. This is the moment to use them. Look at your left column and ask yourself:
What are the things I did during the conversation that I know see led me to frustration and loss of opportunities?
Did I live my opinions as such? Or did I consider them observations?
Did I appropriate my judgments?
Did I explore the mutual interest? Did I clearly manifest it?
Did I back my opinions on recurrent observations of the past?
Were all these true observations? Did I check it with my interlocutor?
Did I inquire productively alongside him/her, attempting to guarantee the truth in my observations?
Am I sure I deeply explored whether those observations were the only ones that could be made about the matter? Or may there have been other facts I ignored?
Did I ask for authorization to express my own expectations about future behavior?
Did I productively inquire about my interlocutor's expectations?

I think I could guess you did not do most of these things. It is time to take courage and do them. If we want to get something other than frustration and distress, we need to take the responsibility of acting differently. Now you can see a set of actions you did not carry out, but you can do now. No matter what the other person does, it is you who wishes to change the course of the conversation. Otherwise, you would not have used it in the exercise. It is your responsibility to act differently. In order not to fall into the trap of, what I like calling, the madness of always taking the same steps, expecting different results for the next time.
If we wish something other than frustration and distress, we have to act differently the next time we have this conversation.

There is time for a final thought: many times, during the course of my workshops or classes, students pose the idea that, given it is very complicated to say what I am thinking, *the way I am thinking it*, at all times, the solution was to "*smooth what I say*, in order to reflect *approximately* what I am thinking, but without hurting the other, so I do not harmed."

But precisely this behavior implies not acting with sincerity, given we should not forget we have said sincerity is "Always making sure our public speech (what I am saying) is IDENTICAL to our private speech (what I am thinking)."
On the other hand, when trying to "smooth" our sayings, what usually happens is we end up saying what we did not want to say, and even worse, cause confusion in our interlocutor many times. I have seen in plenty occasions how someone wanted to make a criticism, but made it in such a "smoothed" way the interlocutor interpreted as a compliment.

Sonia is the administration manager of the company Carl works in. She is not satisfied at all with how he works. Sonia thinks Carl is very unorganized and that makes him completely inefficient. She is willing to fire him if Carl does not improve his performance.

Before taking the decision of firing him, Sonia decides to give him one last chance.
She is willing to tell Carl she is not satisfied with how he works and he needs to improve if he wants to keep his place.
But, it turns out Sonia does not want to hurt Carl (because she is sure he is a good person), nor she wants to argue with him. Then, she decides to "smooth things a little". She wants to tell him about her dissatisfaction and about the danger of not improving his performance, but she does not want to cause an argument.
Then, the dialogue goes like this:

SONIA: "Carl, I want to speak with you for a minute."
CARL: "Of course, Sonia. It is my pleasure. I'm listening."

S: "Look, Carl, you are a good employee. Mostly, you have great values and we all appreciate you. However, I wanted to tell you I have noticed your work is a bit disorganized, and that may end up affecting your productivity. It would be really nice you improved this aspect a bit."
E: "Of course Sonia, I will. Thank you very much!"

Sonia wanted to tell him she was not satisfied with Carl's work and he needed to improve it to keep his job. Nonetheless, in order to "smooth it" she said it would be really nice if he improved how organized he was. Further, she told him everyone appreciated him and he was a person with great values.

Clearly, in her attempt to "smooth things a little", Sonia DID NOT tell him what she really thought. Her public speech (what she told Carl) was different from her private speech (what she thought while she was telling him).

And, even worse, Carl left the meeting thinking something other than what Sonia wanted him to.

We realize about this when Carl meets John in the elevator, and tells him:

CARL: "I just had a small talk with Sonia."
JOHN: "So? Was she mad?"
C: "No, not at all! She told me she appreciates me a lot and she knew I have great values. In the end she told me to be more organized. Luckily, it seems she is very pleased with me!"

The real solution, as we have seen on this chapter, does not lie in "changing what I say", but in something much deeper and mature: "Changing what I think", using all the tools the ability of the art of saying the truth puts on our hands.

Changing what I think, seeing opinions as opinions, being willing to accept they can change, and not "disguising" what I say, will let us say what we really think, without hurting or getting harmed.

This way, we accomplish the double purpose of acting honoring a value we consider important, while we obtain the results we were looking for.

We have checked together the importance of sincere communication. While doing this, we could see, or at least I hope so, that in order to be better people it is not enough to claim a list of values, but it is also necessary to carry them out through the virtues of behavior. And, to achieve this last thing, it is indispensable to have the abilities that allow concrete actions.

Values, virtues and abilities. The triple key to open the door to a better world.

**Epilogue**

The man stayed alone. It was not raining anymore.
Suddenly, it was not late anymore. In any case, the night was the marvelous promise of an inexorable and beautiful sunrise. He could still hear in his head the woman's last words: "Your soul is too big to keep it closed, and has too many things to say to keep it shut."

Then, he knew there was a lot to do. Much to try, and much to learn. But, the first steps had been taken. Under the wing of that strange but amazing woman.

He stayed in silence a bit longer. He paid his check and went out to the street. The first lights of the day began to shine over a world filled with new possibilities.

# Chapter 6
**Student Loving** (Today, a promise. Tomorrow, a betrayal)

*-I brought some flowers* – says Miss Kenton when entering the small reading room.
James Steven, better known as Mr. Stevens, the main butler at Darlington Hall, stops reading his book for a moment.
Next, one of the best scenes from a memorable film, *The Remains of the Day*.
This is a film that lets us notice the word's transformative power, and it is not because what is said during its development, but due to what it is not said.
The scene I was referring to is, perhaps, the one that best expresses this absence of conversations. Mr. Stevens loves Miss Kenton. Miss Kenton loves Mr. Stevens. But, neither of them says so. They just focus their attention on the book James is reading. They say what they do not think, and they shut what they feel. Only during a brief moment Miss Kenton dears to insinuate her emotions. But, she does not fall through with it, and submits to silence once again. And, nothing happens. Life gives them an opportunity they do not take. Finally, they both wither living insignificant lives, wishing what they lost, weeping what they could have done but never did.

I must say *The Remains of the Day*, produced in 1993, starring Anthony Hopkins and Emma Thompson, is one of my favorite films. Besides the amazing acting by these two "sacred monsters", every time I watch it, it does not seize to amaze me for its extraordinary showing of the power in conversations. As I have said, on this case, expressed in the absence of such. What is never said plays a main role. There are declarations missing, petitions, and promises. And life begins to take a path these absences show.

There is no doubt our own declarations, petitions, offers and promises mark our path in life. As my dearest friend, the unforgettable Elio Aprile, used to say: "Think what would have happened to your lives if every time you said NO, you had said yes, and every time you said YES, you had said NO."

On previous chapters we have already talked about declarations. This is the moment to finish our exploration about the word's transformative power, focusing our attention on a type of conversation that cannot be absent. If it is missing, things will never happen they way we want them to. Lets discover, together, the power of petitions, offers and promises.

**Commitment management**

We have already mentioned Murray Rothbard. One of my favorite phrases belonging to him is the one that talks about the strong need human beings have to make sense of our actions.
Undoubtedly, this necessity is closely related to the permanent future projection we live in. We seek at all times to find the best way, given our mental models and abilities, to take care of our necessities, interests and concerns.
Multiples times we find our competence or the resources we have are not enough to reach the results we want. In those situations we realize that, in order to take care of our interests, we need other people's help. But, to get it, we need to have an ability: the capacity of managing our commitments, this is the competence to make petitions, offers and promises effectively.

**Steps in an action conversation**

We said we are to explore the last step in the exploration of the word's power, to end up in concrete actions aiming to reach our objectives.
The way of transforming these commitments into concrete actions is by organizing them with the shape of petitions, offers and effective promises. This way, we move on to the action conversation.

**Petitions**
The complete way to express a petition is:

**I ask you to do X with the satisfaction conditions Y**

Of course, we are not saying all petitions need to adjust to this formula. Quite contrarily, the vast majority of the petitions we make and receive on our daily lives are not expressed this way. Here, we present it in its complete way, with an exclusively didactic end. I would like to point out the important aspect of the petition is not its look, but whether it made things happen according to the whomever emitted it wished.

In order to understand the components of an effective petition, lets check them one by one.

1. The **Speaker**. He is the petition's main character, who has a necessity and needs to satisfy it seeking for help. The speaker is the one that wishes an action is carried out, but is not willing to carry it out him/herself (either because he/she does not want it, or thinks he/she lacks the competence, or because he/she does not have the resources).
2. The **Listener**. It is the individual receiving the petition. It is who carries out the corresponding action (in case of accepting the petition).
3. **Action**. Every effective petition involves an action that needs to be carried out. It is precisely this action the main objective of the petition. The action is called to change the state of the situation, making the world adjust to the speaker's desires and necessities.
4. **Interest**. In our formula, it is represented by the letter X. While the action is the petition's objective, the interest is what the action takes care of. For example, in the petition, "Please, buy me an ice cream", the action is buying, while the interest (what the speaker is lacking) is the satisfaction or pleasure to eat ice cream. As petitions take care of more complex necessities, the need to explain the interest motivating the petition increases.
5. **Satisfaction Conditions**. Everything that highlights the petition, which makes it unique and clear. Some examples for satisfaction conditions are: the date, time, place, time consumed, legal matters, etc.

6. **Obviousness Framework.** Everything that does not need to be explained composes the obviousness framework. It depends on the interrelation stories between the speaker and the listener. In a company, the obviousness framework is commonly known as the Firm's Culture.
7. **Context Invariability.** The petition will keep its satisfaction conditions given the context in which the petition was made, does not change significantly. Given "change significantly" is an opinion, it is indispensable to explicit under what context conditions the petition is no longer needed, or new satisfaction conditions should be set.
8. **Trust Framework.**

Trust is based on two opinions:
1. The opinion of competence of whom is destined to carry out and take responsibility of the desired action.
2. The opinion of the values leading the actions carried out by whom takes responsibility to comply.

In order to achieve an adequate Trust Framework, a third opinion is added to these two the Speaker has regarded to the Listener. But, this third opinion is entitled to the Listener rather than the Speaker: The listener's opinion of whether the task to be carried out is truly needed and currently lacking. The Listener judges the Speaker's honesty.

When we see things are not happening the way we want them to, or when we perceive recurrent difficulties in the domain of effective petitions, it is very useful to check each of the components in a petition, and analyze if one of them is lacking or not being properly applied.

**Offers**

To coordinate actions, asking is not enough. On the constant exchange of value for value, we need to have the ability of making petitions to get what we want, and the ability of proposing attractive offers. The basis of Marketing, for example, is supported on the capacity of making effective offers in the market.

Offers take the shape:

**I offer you doing X with the satisfaction conditions Y**

Even though the components of the effective offers are the same as the petitions, the difference is the speaker not only realizes the linguistic action (offering) but also is committed to carry out the involved action (in case the listener accepts the offer).

Then, it is important to note that in an offer (unlike a petition) the speaker is the one who wishes the action is carried out, and IS willing to do it him/herself (because he/she wants to, because he/she thinks capable and possesses the resources).

**Promises**

Promises compose the closure of an effective action conversation. It is crucial to have in mind we should never finish an action conversation without checking it has ended with one (or multiple) promises.

A promise is the base of action coordination, and main element to generate trust spaces. Thus, the way in which someone manages his promises tells a lot about his character. Whoever loses the capacity to make promises (because everyone else does not trust his word), loses the possibility to coordinate actions. If this happens with a company's identity, it quickly disappears from the market.

The complete shape of a promise is:

**I promise you I will do X with the satisfaction conditions Y**

Just like with offers, in promises, the speaker is the one committing with the listener to carry out the action. The listener's role is to pay attention to make sure the promise is fulfilled, and being willing to make the corresponding claim in the case the satisfaction conditions delivered by the speaker are not the ones agreed upon originally.

This way, we have checked the abilities that allow designing actions and implementing their effective coordination.
As it happens with every discipline, so that it does not remain merely as a good intention, it needs to be carried out recurrently.
At first, it will not be easy. But, if the participants keep the apprentice's high spirit and the protagonist's ethic, they will find, little by little, the results of their task in common improve noticeably, the relationships become stronger and each of them experience the pride of taking care, unconditionally, of the commitment with their actions and the responsibility of the consequences of their actions.
And, as we become more competent in managing our commitments, we will be in better conditions of noticing a phenomenon that happens to be decisive to build a team, form a family or participate in a group of friends: the phenomenon of trust.

## Trust

Trust is the main element in relationships between individuals. Without trust, it would be impossible to coordinate actions with other people. Many times, we do not see our daily life is based on trust opinions we have on people around us, and the trust opinions people around us have about us.

Understanding trust is understanding it represents two sides of the same coin. Each of us needs:
   a) Having grounded trust opinions about other people
   b) Achieving other people can ground positive trust opinions about us

Ergo, when it comes to trust, we need to learn how to trust others and we need to get other people to trust us.
If we fail in either aspect, our possibilities diminish drastically.

Being trust an emotion or state of mind unchained by an opinion, it is better not to forget these always have a temporal structure. They are said at a present, by an observer taking care about a future that concerns or interests him, and backing on his past experiences.

Opinions, or judgments, are inventions, articulations built by an observer based on his past experiences, backing on the ones he chooses to highlight to support the opinions he articulates. As a consequence of having this temporal structure, given it originates in an opinion or judgment, trust is subject to change. Even though the past cannot change, the articulation or interpretation we make about the past can. And, with the new interpretations rise the changes in opinions.

Then, trust, as an emotion, is generated by an opinion, exposed to breaks.

The emotion of trust can refer to a person, a group of people, a society, or oneself. In every case, trust has three dimensions.

1) **The Ethics and Values dimension**. Opinions are founded in actions. In the case of judgments about personal values, the opinion about the coherence between the public speech (whatever the individual says, claims or declares), the private speech (whatever he thinks) and whatever he effectively does is at stake. Only when we can make the observation about recurrent actions that allow articulating that coherence exists, we ought to argue we have a grounded opinion about the ethics of an individual or a group of them. The values we usually focus our attention on are those related to what we call Sincerity, Honesty, Dignity and Integrity.

2) **The Ability, Capacity or Effectiveness dimension**. Here, the competence an individual that is being judged has to complete a task is analyzed. Abilities are explored as much as the satisfaction conditions involved, the expectations about what is desirable that determine the quality standards we operate on when coordinating actions and the possibilities we have, individually and collectively to take care of the proposed situation.

3) **The Commitment Management dimension**. At this point, we analyze the manifested ability to comply as

promised. Despite sincerity and ability, we need to know the individual's story of interrelations, in order to have a grounded opinion about how he honors his word.

In critical situations, trust becomes a great possibility. It will help us to effectively trust others (which we will need to know how to ground our judgments supporting why we trust others) as much as to get others to trust us (constantly showing them actions allowing them to ground positive opinions about how we acted on the sincerity, ability and commitment management dimension).

Further, trust is one of the great engines for human actions. Humans relate to each other, basically, based on two emotions: trust or fear.

Thus, when we are not competent to trust or generate trust, our only alternative is the threat fear generates.

It is right to claim fear works. The fatal inconvenient it presents is, given people get used to their pain threshold, it is necessary to increase the threats' level so that it "keeps working". Repression must become more intense each time, increasing its cost. Finally, it ends up breaking down due to its own weight.

Trust, on the other hand, is the basic foundation for every human relationship that is not based on fear or strength. When the action coordination and cooperation lean on trust, power rises based on the authority that is not backed on strength. There are multiple sources of authority (moral characteristics, competence or ability, wisdom, age, love, respect, money, etc.) but all of them follow the same purpose: provide power, the capacity to generate effective actions within a certain domain. It is wonderful that in trust relationships, this power is conferred, deposited on someone (or a group of people) by those who that power is going to be used on. This kind of relationship is the one we see between parents and their children, doctors and their patients, a couple or a family, teammates, or employees in a company.

It is important to notice a trust relationship does not need to be a relationship in which power is symmetrical. Many trust relationships seen in a company, for example, are totally asymmetrical regarding power. But, since this power is conferred by someone that power applied on, this relationship absolutely respects the dignity of the people involved.
The conferred power it is always subject to be removed. The criterion used to give and remove it is, precisely, trust.
Likewise, trust is the answer we have found as human beings for the challenge of permanently living under contingence and unpredictability conditions. Without the capacity to trust, and doing it with solid arguments, human beings become extremely vulnerable. To face the challenges life sets before us, we need to trust. We need to trust ourselves (self-confidence) and others. If we are capable of experiencing trust, we become self-confident, more powerful, and less vulnerable.
When we say someone generates trust, we are claiming we think that person "will know how to take care of me", my interests, and concerns, and he / she will take all of it into account when taking actions.
When we trust, we make a bet. As it is based on opinions, trust always aims towards the future. And, anything we say about the future will always be an opinion (more, or less, grounded; but always an opinion); never an observation. Since it is a bet, nothing guarantees the results from trusting. We can barely add elements whether to bet or not. Bur, in any case, the bet will be a decisive one. Many times, our lives depend on it.

One of the most impressive learning experiences I have had giving seminars and courses, happened during a set of workshops I led in Spain, for the Spanish Civil Guard (a high military elite group). I remember I was finishing the presentation about the three dimensions of trust, when one of the officers stoop up and told me something I will never forget:

-"César, when you talk about trust, you are referring to one of the most important subjects us, Civil Guards, have on our daily basis. Because, every day, I am putting my life on my partners' hands. I trust them, and they trust me. And that is the only way to keep each other alive. Imagine, for example, at the barracks planning our movements for the following night. So, I tell Paco (another partner, who was present at the workshop): "Paco, you cover me", and Paco promises he will. From then on, my life depends on my trust in Paco. And that's the way it is, given if later, when in battle, I hesitate for a moment, if, for an instant, I'm not sure whether he's taking care of me, and I turn around to check if he is there; even if Paco is there covering me, I do not go back home alive that night."

That is the nature of human relationships. It is not enough for "Paco to be there". That is a necessary, but not exclusive, condition. In order to stay alive, we need "Paco to be there" and we have to remain absolutely convinced "Paco is there". If we live by those rules, we will live with trust. And trust is the biggest threat for vulnerability and fear.

Trust, as much as the lack of it, predispose us for action. But, the actions trust predisposes us to are quite different to those encouraged by its absence. Living in a trust context gives us the possibility to enjoy each moment in our lives a little more. It makes us more optimistic towards the future. It lets us, as Joan Manuel Serrat says, feel "we can walk distracted through life without being in danger".

Distrust prioritizes actions focusing in conservation, protection and security. When operating based on distrust, we take shelter, hide, cling to our belongings, we do not delegate. Trust, on the other hand, promotes the actions leading to transformation, creativity, the opening a new possibilities. Based on trust, we expose ourselves, we let others do, we delegate effectively. Like Rafael Echeverría says: "Trust happens to be the greatest engine for action and, particularly, for the potential transformation in human beings."

We have said trust involves the necessary abilities to ground opinions about other people's ethics and competence (which is why we trust others to delegate on them part of our interests), as much as the competence to get others to have positive opinions about our ethics and abilities to take care of their interests, in such a way they find it effective to delegate their interests on us. Those are the two sides of the same coin: the valuable coin of trust.

The second aspect about trust reminds us we all have a "public identity". Given we are human beings that interact with other human beings, we cannot stop, precisely during the course of those interactions, others from having an opinion about us. What is relevant for us is others will interact with us based, for that interaction, on the trust opinions (positive or negative) they might have about us. We cannot stop that from happening. Human beings always act based on our own opinions. To make this matter even more complicated, these opinions might be either grounded or ungrounded. But, in any case, they will be the motive pushing the choice others might make when coordinating actions with us, or not.

Needless is to say this choice other people make will be decisive to determine our success, viability and happiness. If people around us have negative opinions about us, EVEN THOUGH THESE MIGHT BE UNGROUNDED, they will not choose us to coordinate actions with. Ostracism is the end result when others people decide not to coordinate actions with us.

Then, it is indispensable to understand completely the nature of this challenge. Realizing we all have, in a way, a certain fame. For the ancient Romans, Fame was one of Jupiter's messenger, who represented the "people's voice". In "The Aeneid", Virgil imagines her living at the Earth's core, surrounded by Credulity, Error, False Joy, Terror, Sedition and False Rumors. She has plenty of eyes and mouths, and flies around at high speeds. Many times, fame is represented as a feminine figure, with huge eagle wings. She can be found over the clouds, carrying a double trumpet in his mouth, meaning she spreads the truth as much as lies. That is how we can see it, for example, represented in a statue at the entrance of the main faculty of Seville University.

Fame's metaphor should catch our attention. We have to know we cannot avoid other people from listening the sound of "Fame's double trumpet", whether we like it or not. Our task is not to avoid it, which would be impossible. Our task is to show people we care about, the proof of our concrete actions. All we can do is taking actions that are both effective (which reflects our ability on the respective action domain) and ethical (consistent with the values we say we prioritize). We cannot but try these concrete actions to be the base of the argument for the opinions other people will use to decide if they will coordinate their actions with us or not.

If I trust others and they trust me too, I will coordinate actions with them. If I trust myself, I will start new companies. In any case, I will change reality. It is about trusting or not trusting. I doing it choosing carefully the arguments, because as Henry Ford said: "If you think you can, as much as you think you cannot; you will be right."

**Trust and conversational abilities**

During my training as a professional Coach, I had the opportunity of learning from the thoughts of one of my greatest teachers, Rafael Echeverría.
Rafael was kind enough to show me the deep relationship between the phenomenon of trust and the competence to talk.
Attempting to help build trust contexts in practice, I transcribe these abilities.

1. Effective listening

There are few things that generate more distrust than talking with someone who seems not to be listening. Effective listening means letting the interlocutor finish his thought without interrupting him, respectfully inquiring his motives, interests and expectations, and constantly verifying the assumptions and beliefs he takes as valid.

2. Making precise observations

Even though we know human beings cannot be "objective" when describing a situation o selecting information, we can (and should, given we want to generate trust) be precise with our observations. Precision does not mean our claim is the only one that can be done given the circumstances, but such observation perfectly adjusts to that portion of reality we want to highlight.

3. Clarity and opportunity in declarations
When taking decisions, when declaring, it is crucial being safe we have authority in the action domain affected by the declaration. Otherwise, the declaration will be invalid. People who constantly formulate invalid declarations do not get to generate trust around them.

4. Solid arguments when giving an opinion
Given opinions seek to reduce unpredictability and contingence, the art of grounding own judgments in a solid way happens to be a very promising ability to build trust spaces. Opinions inspired by a clear interest, which are backed on true and relevant observations, based on expectations adequately communicated and restricted to a certain action domain, are a powerful source to generate trust.

5. Responsibility when offering, asking and promising
The competence to manage commitments and taking care of unexpected situations that may rise when carrying out certain actions, taking responsibility for the results of those actions, is a decisive ability too, when it comes to building spaces of mutual trust.

**The Great Seagull spirit**

To round up, I would like to present a few paragraphs to mark the importance of learning how to manage commitments. Knowing how to ask, offering, or promising, goes beyond effectiveness. Of course, effectiveness is valuable and it is worth making the effort to reach every day a greater level of effectiveness in our tasks.
But, we would be wrong if we think commitment management is one of those "popular" courses of our current time, which are promoted something like this: *"Do you want to be more*

*effective? Then, make effective petitions! And you'll see the world at your feet."*

Learning how to ask, offer and promise is learning to make things happen. It is realizing if we do not ask for what we want, nobody in the world has the obligation to give it to us, or even know we need it.
It is understanding completely an offer might be missing to fulfill our dreams. An offer we make can be the first step of a road leading to happiness.
It is realizing promises are the material our identity builds upon. Complying with our word still is a virtue, even in the midst of the changing times.

I still remember a phrase one of my masters told me when I went for the first time to a workshop to learn about human communication: "They believe they barely come here to learn how to communicate. But, they don't know they are coming to free the Great Seagull spirit sleeping inside them."

Perhaps, it is time for you to free that spirit and start to fly.

# Chapter 7
## Young Men of Honor
By Alan Grinstein

*Chief Brashear: "Forgive me sir, but to me, the Navy isn't a business. It's an organization of people who represent the finest aspects of our nation. We have many traditions. In my career, I have encountered most of them. Some are good, some bad. However, I would not be here today if it weren't for our greatest tradition of all."*

*Captain Hanks: "And which one is that?"*

*Chief Brashear: "Honor, sir."*

This is an abstract from the final scene in *Men of Honor*. The film, directed by George Tillman Jr., was released in 2000. Starring Robert De Niro and Cuba Gooding Jr., the movie tells the story of Carl Brashear, who attempts to become the first African American Navy Diver while his extremely exigent trainer, Master Chief Sunday, desires to see him fail.

On this scene, Chief Brashear asks in front of a Committee to be reinstated in the Navy despite having a prosthetic leg. The hearing's chairman, Captain Hanks, hesitates to grant him his petition so he submits him to the twelve steps test. With tremendous effort, Chief Brashear accomplishes to take twelve steps while wearing the newest diving suit, so Captain Hanks has no other choice but to order his immediate reinstatement in the Navy.

At a certain point, Chief Brashear takes a misstep that puts him in a bad spot, on the verge of failing such test. However, he comes through, and all thanks to the one trait Brashear would never be willing to give up: honor.

Honor is the theme that drives this chapter. As is honor the reason why I decided to study in Washington and Lee University. The tale of my experience at W&L will, I hope, serve as en example of why it is crucial to generate an environment of honor and trust in the workplace.

Washington and Lee is a Liberal Arts university located in Lexington, Virginia. From the moment I heard about it, back when I was in my junior year in high school, I knew that it was the college where I wanted to go to. The application process was a long and stressful one. During that process, I remember constantly, incessantly being reminded of the importance of the university's honor code. Every time I met with the Dean of Admissions, the honor code was the very first matter brought up in conversation. It is the university's duty and purpose to stress each of its applicants on the significance of such honor code. I remember being told many different stories on how students respected this honor code. I also recall being warned of the policy on breaking the code: "one strike, you are out."

The day came when I finally arrived at Washington and Lee. I could not believe my eyes for witnessing the place I had been looking at in pictures for two years. After a quick tour around the university, the pre-orientation week schedule began taking over my plans. Since I was an international student, I had to be at the university prior to the rest of the first-year students to be familiarized with the culture and traditions. Logically, the honor code was the main focus our advisors kept weighting on. Then, in a meeting at which all the international students were present, we were told about the signature of The White Book. This was the book in which the honor code was explained in detail. We were not officially enrolled in the university until we signed the book, agreeing to comply with its demands. "No cheating, lying or stealing" is the founding pillar the honor code stands on. Signing the book meant we acknowledged it was the university's right to expel anyone who broke the honor code, and nobody could start his or her classes without signing it.

Couple days before classes began, I walked with some friends towards the Lee Chapel, where the book was placed. There was a long line of students signing the book and one could experience that feeling we all have before taking that step that will be life changing. That signature put us all, the students, on the same page, as equals, as gentlemen and ladies of a community agreeing to abide by the rules, respecting each other, respecting the honor code. I will always remember that moment where I held the pen, while my hands were shaking, and started drawing my signature below the names of my fellow students. Then I felt relieved; finally I was part of the community I so eagerly had been looking at for the previous two years.

The Honor Code is the sacred glue that holds the community together. Each student respects it because, first, they know the person next to them respects it as well and, second, if they get caught breaking it, they will suffer the consequences. Respecting the honor code meant living by three rules:

1. **No cheating.** Every student is committed to never cheating on any exam, paper or project. Any external, unacknowledged aid is prohibited and results in an investigation the university carries out, leading to expelling the student. Every student has to sign the honor code on each assignment, otherwise becomes invalid, writing the following sentence: "On my honor, I have neither given nor received any unacknowledged aid on this exam/paper/assignment."
2. **No lying.** Each student is expected to tell the truth regarding university matters at all times. Lying to any authority also leads to getting expelled.
3. **No stealing.** Students cannot take someone else's property without consent. If one does, the university expels the student as well.

Further, every person in the community takes the oath to report whomever they catch breaking the honor code to the Executive Committee. Then, the EC calls the student who has allegedly broke the honor code and evaluates the situation. If proven guilty, the student has two options: leave the university by his or her own means as if she or he dropped out, or request for a trial.

Every member of the community is invited to assist to the trial, which is, as you can imagine, a very stressful situation for the accused student. This is the student's last chance to argue for his or her innocence. If, once again, found guilty, the student gets immediately expelled from the university. In order to avoid this tense, but fair, position, students choose to respect the honor code, everyday.

Besides being the most appreciated tradition for its uniqueness and the sense of fellowship it generates, the honor code brings tremendous benefits for the community.

First of all, the honor code creates a safer environment around campus. Since fewer students are tempted to steal or behave inappropriately, few Public Safety officers are needed to patrol. Thus, less capital needs to be allocated for that matter. Such capital can be more productively used for constructing new buildings around campus, or renovate old ones, for example, or offer more classes, hire new and qualified professors, increase financial aid, and buy the newest technology both for entertainment and educational purposes. Overall, it leads to a more complete, better experience. In my four years at school, I kept constantly noticing progress and improvement around campus.

Second, the honor code makes it easier for students to manage their time more efficiently. It is common for students to be stressed out about all the assignments they ought to complete for their classes. This stress usually behaves like an exponential equation around midterms or final exams. At Washington and Lee, in many cases, students are given the chance to take their exams on their own. That is, they can take exams in their dorms, at the library or wherever they feel more comfortable, at any time they desire before the deadline, instead of having to plan on being in classroom 302 of the Business Department at 8pm, sharp. This is possible due to the confidence level professors are encouraged to practice with their students. Students behave as if they were taking the exam in class, surrounded by their classmates; while actually sitting by themselves in the library at the time they see more fit to take the exam. This allows them to build their schedules more freely, not worrying about being obliged to take their tests on a specific place at a certain time. Further, on scheduled exams students are required to attend, professors do not need to be present, checking on them. They can be working their office hours in case students from other classes, or even those taking the exam, need help with their assignments, leading to more productivity.

The honor system motivates students to trust each other: trust no one will cheat, that when the time comes to prove their knowledge, everyone will be in the same position and nobody will have the advantage of being further away from the professor, making it easier to take a peak of their class notes.

The honor code encourages students to bring out the best of themselves, to study more to do better because the person next to them will have done the same to get better grades. Healthy competition.

Why is this chapter relevant for this book's mission? Because, as businessmen, entrepreneurs, managers, directors, we need to create a work environment in which trust is promoted. We accomplish to trust those working around us when everyone honors their commitments.

Trusting your co-workers reduces costs, since a boss who trusts his workers can skip certain process controls. Another way in which trust reduces costs is by saving time. Time is money, and if a boss can increase productivity by delegating on more subordinates, instead of having to do a task him/herself, then more tasks can be done at the same time. Further, although this is harder to measure accurately, trust generates responsibility on each worker. Psychologically, it generates a positive impact, as the worker feels appreciated within the company. Not having a superior controlling your every move is a reason to feel happy and proud; thus, it motivates workers to perform better at their jobs.

Trust is a much more useful tool than fear, which aims to reach the same results but ultimately accomplishes quite the opposite ones. As a boss, leave fear behind, it will only generate misery. Start building environments where trust reigns the floor.

~ o ~

## A few words on Young Men of Honor
By César Grinstein

When I asked Alan to make the tremendous effort (mental as well as physical) of translating to English many of the texts composing my two first books, it had never crossed my mind we were starting a literary adventure that would result in a brand new piece. Getting Acquainted is, without a doubt, a book itself. Although it keeps the main ideas and the spirit of ConVersar and Abracadabra, it is the result (improved, I hope) of the passing of time, the reflection it involves, and the refreshing buoyancy of the juvenile mind.

As Alan moved on from one text to another, we reflected together about the new ways of saying what I had already said, and better examples to expand the comprehension and learning that could result from my older attempts as a "lonely" writer. I must confess the questions my son brought up along his voyage through this turbulent sea of words filled me with pride and satisfaction. Let me assure you Alan deserves most of the credit, since he constantly tried to respect what his father had wanted to write and explain, whilst proposing new (and better) ways of expressing it.

Reaching the end of the road, I believed that work had to be acknowledged and rewarded. So, I asked him to write a chapter of his own. In a way, I wanted this shared job to serve as a sort of "baton passing", now that I have travelled most my path and he is just beginning his.

We agreed narrating his experience at WLU was an appropriate ending. And there are various reasons to justify it.

First, the entire process which Alan had to go through to get admitted and his scholarship was a hard job we also carried out together. While trying to get admitted, Alejandra, Alan and I went through every imaginable state of mind. Hope, doubt, fear, enthusiasm, uncertainty, and, finally, joy, were all the emotional dressings of this project.

Second, those four years away from home were an incredible learning opportunity for our small family. For Alejandra, his mother, Kevin, his older brother, and me. Knowing we were doing the right thing, while the long distance kept crushing our hearts was a litmus test.

These two first reasons lead to a third one, final corollary justifying the narration of the experience: We are sure, besides the technical abilities Alan might have acquired in Lexington, the fact of having lived under the figure of the Honor Code is the greatest learning opportunity a parent can wish for a child.

Young Men of Honor highlights the importance of values. And, one cannot live a worthy life without respecting a set of values. Just like Ulises tied himself to the mast of his ship so he did not fall for the mermaids' singing, each of us must grab on, immovable, to that set of values conforming our personal ethics.

The reader may remember the definition of intelligence I proposed in the Introduction of this book, which is an ability to a) make distinctions in a determined domain of action, b) putting those distinctions in order to obtain the achievements proposed, c) while respecting the values composing the life ethics we wish to honor.

We also said intelligence demands the presence of values. Without them, we can aspire to cunning, but never intelligence. Cunning is intelligence stripped of values.

Intelligence is that ray of humanity that differentiates us from beasts. It is the guide that governs the human spirit.

Constructing a community based on the Honor Code is the greatest challenge, and the greatest hope. For ourselves, for our families, for our companies, and for our societies.

An Honor Code makes life simpler, the coordination of actions more fluid, the cost of productions lower, productivity higher. In few words, it produces abundance. Both material and spiritual.

Wherever Honor becomes the code leading every action, we will have a group of worthy women and men. A community of intelligent people, peaceful and productive, with no intentions to harm each other, cheat each other, betray each other. And, in that way, whether it is on Washington and Lee's campus, or companies' buildings and factories, or in the intimacy of our homes, we will be constructing a space in which we can practice the greatest of human rights: the pursuit of own happiness.

# Epilogue
## And nothing else matters

It was the year 1819, and the General San Martín saw that his Continental Plan for South America's independence was in trouble. Political matters coming from Santiago de Chile and Buenos Aires kept his Andes Army practically immobilized. Logically, morale was beginning to drop within his troops. It was then when he came up with the famous Andes Army Proclaim. In it, a motivated San Martín speaks about the dangers approaching the Revolution and encourages his troops to continue fighting as they could. He says that if there had not been any money, meat and tobacco would not lack. And if there were no more clothes, not even the "baizes" made by their wives, "we will walk bare-naked, like our countrymen, the Indians."
The only important matter was not to give up the fight. And that is how the "Libertador" expressed it.
But, in the Proclaim, there is a phrase that is moving, that shows the core of the "sanmartinian" thinking and, I believe, should make an impact on everyone loving life and opportunities it offers:

"Lets be free, and nothing else matters."

This petition to be free and the declaration that nothing else matters at all compose my life's fundamental value. I am completely sure everything else (fortune, achievements, rewards, even health) lack sense if we cannot enjoy and practice the only natural right I consider we have as humans: living free, choosing how to do it, where to do it and with whom.
I believe even love crumbles if not free. Because, being love the most sublime expression of the human soul and conscience, it can only fully exist in a soul and conscience that are, primarily, free. Only the free man or woman can fully love. Because love is not an emotion we can experience in solitude. Love needs of an interaction with no limits further than our moral, it nurtures from sharing the existence with the loved one in order to, effectively, love him/her. Without

freedom to be together, love is just a theory. Love without freedom is just a wish. It is wish, but no action.
Loving is being able to choose, while accepting others' choices. And being able to choose is the basic condition for unconditional freedom. When we love, our love's object is the person and the values that person represents for us. But, without the freedom of choosing, it is impossible to choose values. We become stoic without freedom. And, with time, incapable of loving.
Without freedom, our spirit is diminished. And, like Coronel Slade says on his final plea in *Scent of a Woman*: "But there is nothing like the sight of an amputated spirit. There's no prosthetic for that."

In history, many men and women lost their lives fighting for freedom. I firmly believe when someone fights for his own freedom, he fights for everyone's freedom. Because that fight reminds us the human being must never be the medium for something or someone. The human being is an end itself. The fight of those men and women for their freedom is the fight to be themselves. Then, it is the fight of everyone with good intentions that live in our world.

"Getting Acquainted", this book that now comes to an end, has made it its purpose to be contribution, humble but the best I could make, for our basic human freedom. The Transformative Power of the Word is one of the most moving strengths to reach and practice freedom. The Power of the Word, practiced with humbleness, compassion and respect, is an invincible weapon to oppose to violence, deceit and prepotency. And even in these supposed modern and civilized times, it is convenient to pay attention to the rise of threats to our personal freedom.

Practicing our freedom is a moral imperative. I would like to remind each of the readers of this book you have made it this far by choice. You could have had not read it, but each of you chose to read it. If you made it this far, it has been as a free man or woman. And I celebrate it is this way. Because we need more readers, more people practicing the freedom of

choosing what to read, to increase the freedom of choosing what to think. Currently, it is likely the fight for our freedom is done on pages of the literature world.
And, sadly, it does not seem to be a fight we are winning.

A few months ago I read a report about how much people read these days. Amongst the many different sorts of data in there, there was one that particularly caught my attention. It was the statistic about the quantity of books read per year in different countries of the world. Someone may argue quantity does not equal quality, but in sight of the magnitude of the numbers I could not but experience a great concern.
Numbers show that Japan is the country with the highest reading activity. On average, people read 9 books a year. On second place, we can find the US, with 8.8 books per year. Our dearest Argentina, my home, appears quite far down the list, with only 0.5 books per year.

These are frightening numbers. In Argentina, an average citizen reads one book in two years.
Therefore, we are forgetting the word. We are no longer discovering new words. And, given human beings think using the words they know, we are diminishing our capacity to think, to reflect. We are becoming less intelligent.

I said the fight for our freedom is being carried out on book pages.
Each book we read, each phrase we highlight, each thought we elaborate is composed in the testimony of our existence. Thinking, reflecting, is what turns us into the kind of living being we are. Dropping lecture means renouncing to the human being's destiny grandeur.
There are fights that need to be had, even though defeat might be its result. We have said a hero's job is not to avoid his destiny, but fulfill it.
As William Wallace once told a bunch of Scottish men fighting for their freedom during the XII Century: "I am William Wallace! And I see a whole army of my countrymen, here in defiance of tyranny. You've come to fight as free men... and free men you are. What would be of us without our

freedom? Yes, they are many and powerful. And we are just a few. What you are going to do? Will you fight? (…) Aye, fight and you may die. Run, and you'll live… at least a while. And dying in your beds, many years from now. But I am sure that you will be willin' to trade ALL the days, from this day to that, for one chance, just one chance, to come back here and tell our enemies that they may take our lives, but they'll never take… OUR FREEDOM!"

So, we have made it this far. Together, you and I. And I appreciate your effort. It is the time to say goodbye and move on with our path. If this book made sense at all, new roads will rise, showing new, nearby horizons.
Here goes my farewell, brimming with wishes: I hope this bunch of ideas helps you to follow your dreams, constantly, and without quitting at all. I hope you enjoy this unique feeling provoked by having your life ahead. Whatever your job or profession, you complete your tasks with pride and patience. Celebrate your successes and learn from your failures, which will be there by need, by will never be definitive. I hope you are brave enough to keep your values whatever happens, and turn your breaks into challenges. Always remember it is possible to create your life just like a work of art. And the greatest works of art are created with ability, of course, but with perseverance above all. Keep in mind, in spite of the deceits you may cross, the world is filled with anonymous heroes trying not to fall into despair.
Allow yourself to dream. Let your dreams be so big they do not let you sleep.
I hope you laugh, and cry, and run, and jump, and sing, every day a little bit.

Lets be free.
And nothing else matters.

# CONTENTS

| | |
|---|---|
| Extensive dedications, small talent | 3 |
| Preface - Words' Power | 7 |
| Introduction | 13 |
| Chapter 1 - Apprentices and Know-it-alls | 29 |
| Chapter 2 - Achilles' Crossroads | 65 |
| Chapter 3 - Living Poets Society | 83 |
| Chapter 4 - At least, that is my point of view | 123 |
| Chapter 5 - The voice of consciousness | 141 |
| Chapter 6 - Student Loving | 179 |
| Chapter 7 - Young Men of Honor | 193 |
| Epilogue - And nothing else matters | 201 |

www.ingramcontent.com/pod-product-compliance
Lightning Source LLC
Chambersburg PA
CBHW051309220526
45468CB00004B/1265